SMART GIRL,
stupid world

CHOOSING RIGHT IN A WORLD GONE WRONG

SARAH SIEGAND

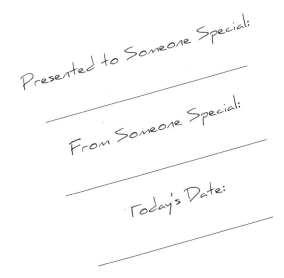

Presented to Someone Special:

_____

From Someone Special:

_____

Today's Date:

_____

Learn more at:
www.smartgirlstupidworld.com

contents

foreword
Pastor Dale Evrist

We live in an age that is rife with people making foolish choices and suffering often devastating consequences. It is extremely painful to watch people live in ways that hurt themselves and others. It is also extremely painful to live with the results of our own foolishness. Sometimes we do it out of environmental conditioning; sometimes ignorance; sometimes fear; sometimes rebellion. But whatever the cause of these bad choices and corresponding consequences, there is a solution; there is a remedy; there is a cure: biblical wisdom.

Wisdom is the ability to know what to do and how to do it. King Solomon said, "Wisdom is the principal thing; therefore get wisdom. And in all your getting, get understanding" (Proverbs 4:7). *Smart Girl, Stupid World* is going to help you to do just that. As you make your way through this thoughtful and straightforward book, you will learn principles of what biblical wisdom is and how to put it into practice in your life. You will also learn how to avoid pathways and pitfalls that lead to unnecessary heartache. You will be challenged to follow the Word, the will, and the ways of God in making every determination in your life, believing that the God who infinitely loves you has a better plan than anything you could conceive of on your own.

Sarah Siegand is a "smart girl." You're going to like her. She is refreshingly honest. She is also refreshingly humble, with a heart of deep compassion for others. She can relate to you. You see, Sarah was not always a "smart girl." When she was a young person, she did lots of not-so-smart things, but she's happy to tell you about them. And as she does, you will get to look into Sarah's past—"warts and all." But you will also get to share in her journey of learning how to walk in God's divine wisdom from above—a journey she is still on every day.

Sarah is a beloved spiritual daughter who I have watched grow into a graced and gifted communicator of light and life. If she comes on a little strong, it's because she loves people too much to not tell them the truth that will set them free. This subject is very important to her—it changed her life. And I'm confident it can change yours, too. So get ready to get smarter, and get ready to grow more and more into the person God created you to be.

Here's to your wisdom journey,

Pastor Dale Evrist
Senior Pastor
New Song Christian Fellowship
Nashville, Tennessee

on the cover
Angela Detweiler

Author's Note: *I want to introduce you to the young lady featured on the cover of this book. Her name is Angela Detweiler, a precious young woman whom I have known for over ten years. Her life and her choices bring honor to the Lord. She does not seek to be known, but to make Christ known. She is a smart girl with a Kingdom purpose! —Sarah*

Angela's thoughts on *Smart Girl, Stupid World...*

In the dictionary, the word "smart" is used to describe someone who is intelligent, sharp, clever, witty, effective, or quick. Being called "smart" is a compliment, a title that sets you apart as someone who is outstanding and likely to succeed. In contrast, we see that the word "stupid" can refer to anything that is foolish, pointless, tediously dull, annoying, troublesome, frivolous, or trivial. Did you grow up like me, thinking "stupid" was a bad word, receiving correction for calling a sibling or friend "stupid" out of anger and frustration? Well, the reality is, some things are just plain STUPID!

There's no way around it. This world can definitely be dull, annoying, and trivial. It can also be unfair; dishing out pain, heartache, grief, and regret in generous servings and always offering second helpings. So many things in this stupid world are way out of our control. We have no say in what family we are born into, the color of our skin, or the ever-frustrating unruliness of our hair.

One of my favorite things about *Smart Girl, Stupid World* is that it lets us in on a little known secret... There is one arena where the choice is all our own. The choice to *get smart*! An option to stand up and shout

9

to this stupid world that we will not take it anymore. There are so many times we feel helpless, but when it comes to the trajectory of our lives, we can make a difference.

In Sarah's book, we are challenged to pursue wisdom. Pursuing something means going after it, which takes a little work and definitely requires action steps. Some of you reading this right now may be thinking, "Well, I'm just not much of a reader, and I don't know if I'm up for all of that..." I encourage you, I'm not much of a reader either, but I read this book cover to cover and I would read it again! Sarah's stories are gripping and raw. She lays it all out there. If you are ready for honest, up-front, vulnerable truth, then look no further. We, as young women, have an opportunity to get smart, get right with God, and get going as the young women we were created to be!

Do you feel trapped by the mistakes of your past? Do you think you have made too many wrong turns to ever get back on the right path? Do you feel your life lacks purpose, direction, or meaning? Guess what? There is hope! This is not the end of your story, your journey, or your life. I would be a completely different person if I did not know God. I would be proud, selfish, lonely, and insecure without the transformation I have experienced in Christ. In Him, I know I am beautiful, loved, valued, significant, and a work in progress.

Sarah writes with compassion and conviction. She knows the pain of a generation of girls who feel unloved, worthless, abused, trapped, and forgotten. She speaks directly to the heart of every girl who feels like her life is going nowhere, fast! Take my word for it, read on. See what happens. As a young woman, I learned so much through reading this book. It leaves you feeling refreshed and empowered. I pray you would see God's hand reaching out to you, ready to pull you up from wherever you are and to set you on the firm ground of a journey with Him. — *Angela*

acknowledgements

There are untold numbers of people who have been an encouragement to me during the many years it took to complete this book. Some of the biggies that deserve the most massive thank you ever are...

Jesse, my wonderful husband, you amaze me with your steadfast commitment to the dreams that God put in my heart. You believed in me even when I wasn't sure if I could keep going. Thank you for the personal sacrifices you've made to make this book a reality. You are a dream releaser, and you make me feel so loved. Judah and Ezra, my blue-eyed boys, you may not have understood why Mommy was so busy with "dat book" she was writing, but my prayer is that someday you will live these pages. There is nothing more important to me than discipling you and training you in the ways of the Lord. Ruthie and Stasia, my precious nieces, you will be the first generation of smart girls with a portion of my very own DNA, and I vow to partner with your parents to help you know Christ and His plan for your life.

Pastor Dale & Joan, you have taught me more than you could ever know about walking more intimately with God and growing in wisdom as His daughter. I deeply respect your leadership and example. Sue, you have been a voice of truth and steady hand to guide me through many tearful afternoons and seasons. Farrar and Betty, you have been a conduit of emotional healing and perspective. Mario, Stacy, and Kay, your prayers are probably the only reason I survived adolescence.

And to the smartest of the smart girls whom I have the privilege of running alongside in this race... Meg, Denise, Kara, Cassidy, Gwen, Janell M., Janelle K., Kari R., Cari B., Danille, Saundra, Heather, Sarah B., your lives and your witness to the world continue to inspire, challenge, and convict me. I am amazed to realize how many Godly friends surround me!

Lindsay, you are the best thing that ever came of "that one project" we worked on together. Thank you for editing this sucker, but mostly for your encouragement and partnership. You have been a great friend.

To Angela and Hannah, thank you for agreeing to put your face to a very high calling of holiness among your generation. You earned that place by your conduct, your humility, and your heart to serve God's purposes through this message.

To Preston and Greg, your vision and your willingness to partner with me to tell this story on screen will never be forgotten... by me or by Heaven! I am blown away by all you invested in this message.

To Patsy, you were a great gift to me as I neared the end of this process. Thank you for your prayers and your encouragement to finish well.

And finally, to my Mary... I dedicate this book to you. You are a living testament of what God can do when we yield our lives to Him. I am proud to call you friend and to be part of your journey as you continue to develop into one very *smart girl*.

introduction

stupid, stupid world

The world we live in, especially as Americans, grows increasingly ridiculous by the day. Television proves this on at least a jillion channels 24–7. The "idols" of pop culture—music superstars, actresses, and billion-dollar heiresses, to name a few—do the stupidest things imaginable, chase counterfeit happiness, and seem to grow more and more popular no matter how they behave. Month-long marriages, teenage plastic surgery, glamorized sexuality; these are just a few examples of the foolishness that surrounds us. Seriously, the world we live in is *stupid*.

Is the answer to such absurdity simply a demand for better behavior? Will wearing geekish solid-color polos and khaki pants for a public school uniform miraculously turn aimless women into fine, upstanding citizens? Can all the savvy advice in *Seventeen* magazine turn anyone into a *smart girl*?

And how does Christianity factor into all of this mess? I mean, if you are a Christian, or at least a churchgoer, don't you just automatically rank higher when it comes to being a good decision-maker? Surely you get bonus points for that, right?

what ever happened to wisdom?

If you haven't figured this out on your own yet, there is no magic wand to get you from the cellars of stupidity to center stage at the ball in a matter of minutes. The only way to become a smart girl while living in this stupid world is to allow wisdom to develop in you, and it happens one moment at a time.

Oh, how I wish I had known that twenty years ago!

When I was a young Christian (in my teenage years especially) I figured if I followed the rules (the *"Thou shalt nots"*), I was probably doing better than most other people my age. Since I was in a home where parents were basically absent most of the time, there was no one to take me by the hand and really mentor me in wisdom. What little bit I caught was from my youth pastors and the parents of other friends who seemed to have it figured out. But most of the time, I was guessing. I made huge choices about my future without having any idea what the will of the Lord was. And I made huge mistakes. I suppose I thought that God's will was for me to be happy, so if what I was doing brought me happiness, I must be in the center of His destiny. Wrong. Soooo wrong.

A few things happened in my young adult life to jar me into repentance. As the clouds of confusing theology parted, it began to dawn on me that despite all of my intellect and honors, I honestly had no idea how to walk in wisdom, and the stakes for my poor choices seemed to be getting higher. I began reading Proverbs every day when I was in college, and I grew more and more convicted, realizing that I had walked very foolishly for most of my life. When I looked around at my peers, Christian and non-Christian, it was obvious I wasn't alone. Foolishness seemed to be the order of the day as we felt our way in the dark, crossing our fingers that we were at least close to being in God's will.

It was in this season that I began asking the Holy Spirit to help me understand what it meant to be a woman of wisdom. Little did I know how much pain and suffering were still on the path to understanding this concept, not only in my own life but in the lives I would become part of.

I have in no way arrived at the end of my quest for wisdom. But I have surely learned a lot over many years about what the Bible has to say concerning why we need wisdom and how we acquire it. I hope to accurately communicate that information to you, along with relevant stories of the stupid world we live in, and humorous details of my own personal failures.

how this book came to be

So... this book took me a heck of a long time to write. It's not because I didn't have anything to say or because I was still confused. When God first laid the idea on my heart years ago, I was so full of passion about the subject matter that I wrote almost the entire thing within the first four months.

And then I moved across the country to an incredible church outside of Nashville, Tennessee. God's perfect plan included me learning more about His ways before I wrote another word. When I finally felt release to work on the book again, I was trying to fit the new things I'd learned into the previous framework, and it was like sewing patches to an old garment. It just didn't jive.

At that same time I dove headlong into my rookie years of motherhood and found my writing would need to wait even longer. Once I cleared the infant and toddler stages, I found the stamina needed to launch into a massive re-write. To my surprise, I still felt the same passion about the subject matter, and I had an even clearer perspective to tell the story God had given me.

This book was conceived through what is known as a "moral imperative," a burdening sense over the state of something that compels you to action. My first few years of volunteer youth ministry leadership led me to tears over and over again as I watched countless young ladies abort their potential and destiny in the Lord through unwise choices. I got to a place where I felt like something *must* be done, and I needed to be a part of that "something."

Mentoring teenagers was part of that "something," but still I found myself frustrated that I wasn't able to fully come alongside them in a way that would systematically repair some of the damage that had already been done. At the time I had no knowledge of or context for discipleship materials like *Freedom in Christ* (by Neil Anderson). I was only able to address things that came to the surface, and there still seemed that there were so many root issues that were undealt-with.

In the midst of this mentoring, my husband expressed a crazy idea out loud one day. We were driving to our little cottage home after a wonderful day in the city—a day where I had poured out my heart to him about the issues that were burdening me concerning the younger generation. He turned to me and said, "You should write a book." *Yeah*. I thought that sounded like a lofty, idealistic way to solve my frustrations.

But that moment stood frozen in time, and I kept coming back to it. I thought of it when I prayed, when I drove, when I was on the treadmill— all the time, basically. Eventually an analogy came my way that beautifully described what was happening to me. The book idea was a cork, and try as I may to push it down under the water, it kept coming up to the surface. God was trying to get my attention. I decided I better listen.

So I set aside my 29th birthday to pray about it and document anything the Lord might tell me. In a matter of minutes, and in what would continue for over four hours, the Lord started downloading a mission, a calling. I knew that until I obeyed it to the end, I would not be able to find resolution to the burden I felt. Truthfully, the burden for this generation still remains, but the fact that I have allowed the Lord to help me sort it out and articulate it in the following ten chapters does bring a certain sense of peace. Maybe now I truly understand what Jesus meant when He said, "Come to Me, all you who labor and are heavy laden, and I will give you rest. Take My yoke upon you and learn from Me, for I am gentle and lowly in heart, and you will find rest for your souls. For My yoke is easy and My burden is light." (Matthew 11:28-30)

What you have in your hand (or on your screen, as the case may be) is a message that I wish I had been given at 16. It is a summation of many lessons I have learned in my pursuit of wisdom (a journey I am still on and always will be). My hope is that other adult leaders who are concerned for young ladies in their lives will find in these pages something to use as a mentorship resource. For the young ladies who wind up reading it without a small group or a leader to partner with, my prayer is that it will inspire them to make Godly choices and to find that accountability for the tough years ahead.

There are many stories in this book, both tragic and uplifting. All of them represent actual events, although many names and specifics may have been deliberately veiled in some instances to protect the privacy of those involved.

so, who is this book for anyway?

Young women are the focus of this message, particularly those who are in the transition years from adolescence to adulthood. I have seen women make a lot of bad choices over the years, but none so monumentally cataclysmic than those which were made during these critical years. Some women never really outgrow the pattern of foolishness, honestly, and some begin the pattern at frighteningly young age. But generally speaking, this is a sound median age range for this book. I purposely put a word of caution on the back cover to help alert parents or leaders to the fact that the message contains mature content, and discretion should be used when recommending this book to readers under the age of 14.

Some people have wondered how the mature issues of sex and such will be handled on the following pages. I'm a pretty frank person, and I've found that teenagers are exposed to all kinds of raw subject matter on the foolish side of life, so it makes the most sense to me that big issues not be tiptoed around when you're taking God's side. I do recommend that parents and leaders read the book before they pass it off to a young lady, so they can assess whether or not she is ready for the content of this book. Some younger teenagers are already in desperate enough situations that the mature subjects need to be addressed immediately. For anyone wondering, I encourage you to use discernment to know who this book is right for, and at what age.

just obey

No matter where this book ends up, read by many or by few, I must concern myself only with the fact that I have obeyed God in writing these pages. One thing I have learned in my pursuit of wisdom is that His way is *always* best. I don't need to finagle my way or convince Him that I know what I'm doing. I really *don't* know what I'm doing unless I have His grace and guidance to direct me. I have to trust Him and believe that He will do what He wants with this work.

"Wisdom is more precious than rubies; nothing you desire can compare with her."
Proverbs 3:15 (NLT)

chapter 1 get smart

stupid is as stupid does

I was barely 17 years old, and boy was I dumb. The fact that I was a good Christian girl who abstained from everything and earned straight A's made my stupidity even more unbelievable. How could a girl with such a promising future find herself hundreds of miles from home, alone with a boy in his bedroom (a boy with not-so-great intentions, mind you), no parents in sight, and all because of an "innocent" lie?

Our high school speech team was at a big out-of-state tournament, and I "innocently" asked my coach if I could stay at my "cousin's" house in that same city, instead of staying with the team at the hotel. My "cousin" wasn't my cousin at all, but a boy named Mike, who I had met at a music camp during the previous summer break. I barely knew him except from a few phone calls and one short visit with two of my girlfriends a few months before.

I know, I know... it looks completely suspicious. Honestly, I had no intentions of doing anything with Mike beyond staying in his family's guest room and eating some of his cereal in the morning. Yes, I was the typical girl who would make youth pastors and parents roll their eyes and say, "Hellooo! What were you thinking?" How could I have missed the likelihood that maybe this boy was expecting something out of the overnight stay? How could I have lied about it in the first place? After all, I was the poster-child for a fine, upstanding young lady. I was a church-going Christian who didn't drink, smoke, or party, and who bragged about my virginity.

Somehow I was oblivious to the idea that Mike wanted to jump me. I know, it's very hard to believe, but I was clueless. Honestly, I just liked the attention he gave me, and I thought spending extra time with him would give me plenty of it. When my "aha!" moment came, I suddenly saw what a dangerous position I had put myself in. Mike and I were sitting on his bed looking at pictures in a photo album, his parents already sound asleep, and he suggested we take a dip in his hot tub.

"I didn't bring a bathing suit," I told him dismissively. And then he just looked at me, uncaring, with a mischievous grin. I finally got it, and then... I totally panicked.

I was caught between feelings of, *How could I be so stupid?* and *I gotta look cool.* My panic stole whatever courage I might have had. Oh how I wish I would have said, "Look, creep, my body is the temple of the Holy Spirit, and you better keep your impure thoughts and intentions to yourself!" Instead, I floundered through some lame excuse about how I didn't think I could do that because some other guy had emotionally scarred me by trying to move too fast. I tried to get the sympathy vote by looking like a poor damsel in distress, but instead I looked—you guessed it—plain stupid! I knew my excuse looked lame. I hated myself for not telling the truth anyway. Thankfully, he got the hint and we both went off to sleep in our separate rooms without so much as a hug. Crisis averted, let the self-loathing begin.

Only after some time did I start to realize what else could have happened that night. What if Mike had started to reach for me? What if he had become forceful? Would I have been able to fend him off? Would I have just given in? After all, even though I definitely did not want to have sex with this boy, I certainly had a level of attraction for him or I wouldn't have lied in order to spend time with him. If he had made further advances, would I have just kept my mouth shut and followed his lead?

That night I barely escaped a potentially dangerous situation, suffering only humiliation. Unfortunately, I know many stories of young ladies who did not escape. Before my mother was married, a similar situation ended in an unplanned pregnancy and a secret adoption. The entire course of a young woman's life can be derailed in moments like these.

The entire course of a young woman's life can be derailed in moments like these.

Sadly, I went on to do many more stupid things throughout my adolescence and young adult years. Most of my stupidity had to do with boys, attention, and relationships. The fact that I survived those years spiritually is nothing short of a miracle to me. Thankfully, I had some great leaders in my life who were praying for me, even though they didn't know all I was dabbling in. (I kept those things secret, of course... Isn't that what all good Christian girls do?)

who cares? nobody's perfect.

So who cares if you make a few mistakes, right? Nobody's perfect—isn't that what we've been taught to believe? While there is truth to that statement, there should be a clear distinction between imperfection and blatant irresponsibility. The way our culture has embraced imperfection as a defense for irresponsibility is grossly over the line.

Only Jesus was perfect. He made a perfect sacrifice for us so that we could be in relationship with God. And that relationship gives us the powerful gift of the Holy Spirit, who reveals what I heard one preacher call "inside information." You don't have to stumble through life when you have the Holy Spirit on the inside of you. He's called the teacher. He wants to coach you through every aspect of your life. He knows the right way to go—always. And His way for us is the way of responsibility.

As awesome as God is, He still doesn't demand perfection from us. That's really helpful for us to know. He isn't an angry God, ready to strike you with an STD if you screw up. He is a loving God who has provided everything you need to keep you safe within His boundaries. We don't carry the weight of being perfect, but we do carry the responsibility of learning and obeying His ways.

I had the opportunity to sit down with a nurse a few years ago who was part of a national research team to develop a vaccine against a prevalent STD in women. She shared with me her background and why this vaccine was so important to her. She had contracted the STD when she was a young adult and shared with me that she would technically have it for the rest of her life. This nurse was articulate, beautiful, and obviously passionate about her work. But within a few minutes I could tell she was living with a completely different paradigm than myself because she

We don't carry the weight of being perfect, but we do carry and the responsibility of learning and obeying His ways.

wasn't a Christian. She said to me that she didn't regret any of the decisions that led her to this place. She felt that those mistakes made her who she is.

It's true—every failure and misstep in life can shape us in some way. And we have the incredible opportunity to learn and grow as a result of our mistakes. Sometimes we learn, sometimes we don't, and history repeats itself. That can be a painful (and deadly) way to live. As Christians, we must face our failures and repent of the sin we have committed in order to be free.

So while it's true that we can all learn from our mistakes, may I suggest to you that there is an even better way to become all God wants you to be?

wisdom is supreme

While God doesn't demand perfection from us, He does command us to gain something really crucial for life: wisdom. Some people think that the best lessons learned in life are learned through mistakes. I disagree. While mistakes can be a powerful teacher, if you plan on learning that way as a rule, you may not live very long.

The Bible clearly teaches God's design for learning wisdom through the model of one generation passing it to the next. In this model, we learn from others' mistakes or successes and apply this wisdom to our own choices. The nurse I met chose to learn from her mistakes, but despite her own personal growth, the STD she has still carries with it grave consequences, like the very real possibility of cervical cancer. Any young woman who heard her story would be wise to take heed and not repeat the same mistakes. It's not about simply getting a vaccine to avoid harmful consequences, it's about the heart issues of obeying God's boundaries and learning from those who have gone before you. That's how God's wisdom works.

Wisdom is knowledge used in the right way. Proverbs 4:7 says that wisdom is supreme. That means it's the most inclusive and greatest thing you could acquire as a believer. Like a supreme pizza, it has everything on it. When you walk in wisdom, you gain many of the things that bring contentment and success, such as emotional stability, financial integrity, and healthy relationships.

Wisdom is knowledge used in the right way.

Solomon was a guy in the Bible who is known for his wisdom. But he had a backstory. He had been raised in a family that was formed in an unusual way for the times he lived in (although it would probably seem very common today). His father was King David, a man who followed God and had a heart after God. But his father also did something really stupid before Solomon was born. King David, a married man, had a one-night-stand with a woman named Bathsheba who was also married to someone else—a dude named Uriah. Bathsheba got pregnant, and David freaked out. As the commander of the army, David sent Uriah to the hottest part of the battlefront, knowing he would be killed. Yep. He was. Then David married Bathsheba and looked like a hero taking care of a poor, pregnant widow.

God saw David's potential and He wasn't going to let that sin go. He sent a prophet to reveal David's sin to him and call him to repentance. It worked! David repented fully but suffered the consequences of losing the child he and Bathsheba had conceived – the baby became ill and died. That same night, a now-repentant David sought to comfort his wife in physical intimacy, and they conceived again. This time the baby was Solomon.

So, needless to say, Solomon was born into some "issues." His parents, as far as we can know, were following God by the time he was born. But no one could erase the circumstances that had brought them together in the first place. Who knows how old Solomon was when he figured it out. But surely there were some awkward conversations at the dinner table along the lines of, "So Dad, how did you and Mom meet?"

Aside from the history of his parents' relationship, there was drama with his brothers and sisters, too. His sister was raped by one of his brothers. And one of the other brothers killed the offender in cold blood because of it. What a mess. What heartbreak. King David saw first-hand what can happen when children don't walk in wisdom.

I do find it interesting that out of all this chaos comes the great King Solomon. Could it be that all the problems in Solomon's family left him longing for a better solution than just learning from mistakes? I believe Solomon wanted to know a better way. And God answered that longing. We have a documented account of the life-changing interaction with the Lord that began Solomon's life-quest for wisdom. It's found in the Bible in 1 Kings 3:5-14.

At Gibeon the LORD appeared to Solomon during the night in a dream, and God said, "Ask for whatever you want me to give you."

Solomon answered, "You have shown great kindness to your servant, my father David, because he was faithful to you and righteous and upright in heart. You have continued this great kindness to him and have given him a son to sit on his throne this very day.

"Now, O LORD my God, you have made your servant king in place of my father David. But I am only a little child and do not know how to carry out my duties. Your servant is here among the people you have chosen, a great people, too numerous to count or number. So give your servant a discerning heart to govern your people and to distinguish between right and wrong. For who is able to govern this great people of yours?"

The Lord was pleased that Solomon had asked for this. So God said to him, "Since you have asked for this and not for long life or wealth for yourself, nor have asked for the death of your enemies but for discernment in administering justice, I will do what you have asked. I will give you a wise and discerning heart, so that there will never have been anyone like you, nor will there ever be. Moreover, I will give you what you have not asked for—both riches and honor—so that in your lifetime you will have no equal among kings. And if you walk in my ways and obey my statutes and commands as David your father did, I will give you a long life."

When Solomon asked for wisdom, he got all of the other things he didn't ask for, like riches, honor, and a long life. I wish I could tell you that Solomon's life continued according to God's will. Unfortunately, he allowed lust and idolatry to lure his heart into sin and willful disobedience to the Lord, proving that wisdom is a daily choice, not a permanent condition.

a parade of failures

When you are young, your experience is limited to the social circles you have first-hand interaction with. As you get older and start to meet people from all walks of life, you get a clearer picture of how stupid our world is. Not to be mean, I'm just sayin.'

When my husband and I started our journey in youth ministry, I was shocked at the stupidity I saw all around me. Not in the teenagers who are just learning how to live life, but in the parents and other adults in the church at large. Parents putting their teenage girls on birth control, buying the alcohol for parties so their kids could "party safe" in a controlled environment, and encouraging their kids to date people they barely know. Huh? These are *Christian* parents?

As I started getting into the lives of these adults and parents, I began learning their own stories. Many were single parents. Many were struggling with their own forms of bondage such as alcohol or sex addiction. Many had never been discipled or poured into intentionally by another older and wiser Christian. They were limping and trying to raise young people in the midst of it. Not exactly a recipe for success.

Your own individual choices directly affect those who come after you, especially your children.

Our churches all over America and the world are filled with people just like this. They didn't set out to make bad choices or set their kids on the world's runway to stupidity. But just because they didn't mean to doesn't make it okay. It has to stop! You can be part of turning the tide. Your own individual choices directly affect those who come after you, especially your children. Now is the time to rise up in wisdom. Otherwise, the failures of previous and current generations will just keep following like the Macy's Thanksgiving Day Parade, mile after mile.

I've met women who seem older than me because of the hardships they've experienced in their lives, only to realize they are actually much younger than me. Many were forced to grow up fast by unplanned pregnancies and a string of bad choices in relationships. Many were abused. Many struggled with drug and alcohol addiction. Many did not have the strength to stand up to the enemy and declare their value in Christ. Now they are trying to raise their own teenagers and feeling confused about where they should be strict and where they should be lenient. But it's not about "house rules." It's about wisdom.

God wants us to pass wisdom from one generation to the next. If you were not on the receiving end of that equation because you were raised by parents who were basically "winging it," then let me encourage you that you can be on the giving end. But you're going to have to determine to live your life on purpose, not randomly.

random living

There is absolutely no way for a young woman to become wise by accident. It just doesn't happen. The Bible says in Proverbs 4:5 that we need to *get* wisdom—that means pursue it to acquire it. We must deliberately go after it, without giving up. We must, like Solomon, pray for it and listen to the Holy Spirit in our daily lives as He imparts it to us. Unlike Solomon, we must hold onto wisdom and never let temptation or sin pry it from our grasp.

The problem is that too many people live life on autopilot. That's certainly the order of the day for American culture. Take life as it comes; see what you think when you get there. It is a very reactive mind-set, instead of a proactive one. I call it random living.

One night when teaching at a church's youth group, I had each of the students draw a card from a normal deck of playing cards. I wanted them to see which card they were choosing so they would get the one they wanted. Then I read a made-up list of each card's value and what that card meant for the student's future. I called out the card and had the students stand who had picked that card. Aces were those who went to college. Two's were those who ended up rich. Nine's were those who ended up divorced, Jacks were those who went to jail and so on. We all had a good laugh at seeing a hypothetical scenario of where people would end up from the card they drew.

The point of the illustration was to illicit an emotional reaction to the unfairness of not being able to choose their own destiny. Well, in fact, they did choose it because they got to pick the card they wanted. But they didn't realize at the time of their choice what that choice meant. If I had read the list of what each card meant at the beginning, they would all have wanted the cards that decided a positive future. They didn't realize what their innocent choice would lead to.

Your life is not a card game, left to chance. Other people do not decide where you end up. While some women suffer horrible acts of abuse and mistreatment that alter the course of their lives beyond their own choosing, those same women have the opportunity to be healed and restored in Christ. That is their choice. God has laid before you a hope, a future, with plans to bless you and bring good things to you (Jeremiah 29:11). It is up to you whether or not you will choose to embrace and walk in that hope.

Those who live randomly, without thought to where they want to end up, will experience the frustration, pain, and fruit of stupidity. Proverbs 1:30-32 basically says that those who won't listen to and learn from wisdom will eat the fruit of their own way on a path that leads to destruction (*Ouch!*).

Statistics say that one-third of the teenagers and young adults who are reading these pages were born into a non-marriage based family.[1] Let's talk straight about it, shall we? The number of unplanned pregnancies equates to millions of children growing up with a nagging lie over them that they were an accident. My husband is an adult on the other side of that. His parents never married each other and have no relationship with one another today. It's a little awkward to explain to my children. But as my kids grow up, they will have many friends who were born into the same situation, so it will not seem foreign to them.

You are not an accident. No matter how randomly your parents may have lived,

You are not an accident. You are here—make the most of it.

35

God still holds a perfect destiny for you to choose. You have been born, like Esther in the Old Testament, for such a time as this. You are here—make the most of it. Allow the Lord to speak to you about your purpose and what you are to do for His Kingdom.

living on purpose

You don't accomplish remarkable things by living a life that is the same as those around you. If you want extraordinary results, you must be willing to make extraordinary sacrifices. What if a young teenage girl is a good swimmer and dreams of swimming in the Olympics? If her dream is only a pipe dream, she can basically do what her peers do... cruise Facebook and text her friends for hours after school, stay out late (doing what??) and eat junk food for breakfast. If she's serious about that dream, however, she will have to sacrifice the lifestyle that most teenagers live.

If you want extraordinary results, you must be willing to make extraordinary sacrifices.

One such teenager won two Olympic gold medals at the 2000 games in Sydney when she was 16 years old. Megan Quann was not a pipe dreamer, she was a teenager who had purpose! Because of that purpose, she knew how to purposefully go after her dream. She knew that if Olympic gold were to be a reality, she would not be afforded the same liberties that others enjoyed. School dances would be substituted with early bed times for an important swim meet in the morning. An afternoon at the movies would be substituted with hours at the pool trying to beat a world record.

What about you? What do you dream of? What purpose does your life have in God's grand scheme of humanity? (Don't you dare say "none!") Some young women have very specific dreams that they hope to accomplish, such as going to college, becoming a doctor, or opening a restaurant. But I've found that most teenagers and young adults have broader and more general dreams in their heart that are not spoken in terms of specifics. Because their dreams seem somewhat vague, they often feel unmotivated to make sacrifices or set goals to accomplish them.

Let me give you an example. Most young women who are Christians hold the dream in their heart to get married someday to an incredible, godly man who loves them. Did you know there are sacrifices involved in that dream just like the dream of going to college? In order to have a lasting marriage with a wonderful guy who loves God (and who can resist that?), you don't just draw the right card out of the deck. It isn't luck that brings that dream to reality. You will have to sacrifice whatever competes for that dream in order to see it come to pass, and it may not happen in your time frame. And if it doesn't, will you still hold on to the dream?

If your dream is to be married to a godly man who loves you, guess what? You have to do it God's way. God is the ultimate Olympic coach. He knows what it will cost you, and He's willing to hold your hand through those sacrifices to get you to the games. In order for your dream to come to pass, you don't get to date whoever you want. You certainly don't get to have sex... with *anybody*. And you may have to pass up some really great guys to get there. And some creeps, too.

Being willing to make sacrifices is part of pursuing wisdom because it keeps the greater picture of your life always in view. Everything is to be held up to the light of who God has called you to be and discarded if it does not reflect His plan. You are not meant to drift from choice to choice, unsure of what to do next. That will lead to stupidity and heartbreak.

You are called to live a life that is purposeful, with His dreams for you in sight, and the road of sacrifice to get there a very present reality. Jesus is our ultimate example, "who for the joy set before him, endured the cross." (Hebrews 12:2)

loopholes, shmoopholes

Living life on purpose and on mission with the dreams God has put in your heart is no easy thing. There will be many distractions along the way, sent by the enemy of your soul to lead you astray and get you to forfeit your destiny. One thing I've seen happen time and again with young people is the deception of "loopholes."

The word *loophole* originated as a term that referred to a gap in a fortified structure, such as a castle. It was where one could hide to defend themselves. Metaphorically, a loophole is a gap, omission, or any ambiguity that can be used for your advantage. In fact, a clear indication that you are using a loophole to mask foolishness is when you're having to defend your choices.

Watch out for any time you may be "technically" following the rules, giving the impression of living in obedience; while in your heart you know you are trying to get around God's boundaries. When I was 18, I had a strong conviction about marrying a Godly man and even had unspoken dreams in my heart about marrying a musician whom I could do music ministry with. Instead of holding out for that person and allowing the Lord to lead me, I used the loophole that my boyfriend at the time went to church and would not interfere with the music dreams in my heart. But was that enough to make Him God's best for me? Nope. And I wasn't God's best for him. And that relationship led both of us away from God's best for a couple of years.

There are loopholes all around you that will pry the dreams out of your hands. Oral sex is a famous one... "It's not intercourse, so it's okay." Really? I could name a dozen girls off the bat who were derailed by the non-intercourse loophole (and these are just girls in my own personal circle!). "Mom said I could spend the night at Sarah's, but Sarah and I wanted to go to Ashley's instead. Isn't it the same thing?" Loopholes reveal unspoken and undealt-with rebellion in your own heart.

I remember explaining to a friend something foolish I did once, but not wanting to admit I was wrong, so I was flowering the story with all kinds of reasons why it might be seen as okay. When I got alone, the Lord said the most interesting thing to me: "Are you trying to convince *Me* you were right? Or are you trying to convince *yourself*?" Ouch. That's called a rebuke, by the way. If you haven't experienced that level of honest love from the Lord yet, I encourage you to not be afraid of it. The Lord disciplines those He loves (Hebrews 12:6).

Loopholes are a trap. Watch out for them—jump over them. Don't exploit them for your own benefit.

small choices matter

Some girls think that as long as you nail the big decisions, small choices don't matter. But all of the big decisions depend on the small ones in ways you may not have considered before. And the seemingly insignificant choices can sabotage you before you realize that a larger choice is at hand.

Take for example Becka. She was 18 years old and just a few months away from realizing her dream of going to college. Becka was a Christian, but she had a history of struggling with drinking when her friends were around. She knew she would have to get victory in Christ over the stronghold of alcohol in order to be accepted into a Christian school (not to mention in order to find peace in her relationship with God). She had been gaining ground through accountability and mentorship and had distanced herself from relationships that led her to compromise in the past. The Christian college Becka applied to knew about her history, and was willing to overlook it since she had been sober for a year and had shown remarkable growth. Happy ending, right? Hold on... the plot thickens.

One day Becka met a new friend at church named Nicole. Nicole was her age and seemed to love God. Becka knew that Nicole had struggled with drugs and alcohol in the past, but she naively looked past that fact. Becka didn't pray about whether she should be friends with Nicole or spend time with her. She didn't talk to anybody older and wiser about whether or not she was strong enough to hang with someone battling the same addiction as her.

After just a few weeks, Becka's friendship with Nicole brought her into a situation she wasn't ready for where others were drinking and pressuring her to do the same. She was ambushed by circumstances she hadn't expected with her new Christian friend. She found herself physically shaking under the spiritual battle raging in her heart as she stared into the eyes of those around her who were inviting her to compromise. Sadly, she succumbed to the pressure and joined them for a drink. Then two... until she lost count.

Ashamed and embarrassed, Becka hid her sin from her parents, her pastors, and the college admissions counselor she interviewed with a few days later who asked her specifically about her sobriety. Eventually, she couldn't take it anymore—she confessed everything and found forgiveness with God and those she had lied to.

But that didn't fix the mess. Becka had to delay her dream of going to that Christian college because of her choice to violate their honor code by drinking and lying. Becka's choices had cost her everything she had been working toward. She would have to grow in her character and in her relationship with God before she could move forward.

Becka's first choice was the smallest and the easiest to make. "Should I hang around with Nicole? Am I strong enough for a relationship with someone who is fighting the same strongholds I am?" This might seem insignificant to most girls. Most would not even think of praying about making a new friend. Jesus wants us to be friends with everyone, right?

What does the Bible say about friends who are a negative influence? "Become wise by walking with the wise; hang out with fools and watch your life fall to pieces." (Proverbs 13:20, MSG) "Bad company corrupts good morals." (I Corinthians 15:33, NASB) Bottom line: choose your friends wisely.

Becka's subsequent choices were much harder. After being put in a situation where alcohol was present, she had a decision to make about whether she would stand, or fall, to the pressure. Unfortunately, standing on her convictions and simply walking away proved to be too difficult. The pull on her life to give in was too strong. And after her failure with that choice, she felt she could not face others with the truth, which led to her choice to lie. Because of Becka's decisions, her immediate future was no longer in her own hands, but in the hands of the college admissions staff who were obligated to uphold their standards of conduct for incoming students.

Small choices matter. And they are the easiest ones to make.

Small choices matter. And they are the easiest ones to make. Handle the small choices well, and you will set yourself up for success when making the big choices.

put it into action

To live a life of wisdom and become the woman God intends you to be, you have to rise above random living and stupidity. Wisdom does not just happen. It does not just "come with age" as the old saying goes. You must deliberately pursue it.

Best-selling author and founder of Freedom in Christ Ministries, Neil Anderson, wrote, "Apart from the Holy Spirit in your life, the greatest power you possess is the power to choose."[2] That means every choice, even a seemingly small one, is important. Every choice should be governed by the question, "What is my God-given purpose in life, and will the result of this choice lead me toward or away from that purpose?" Always remember, wisdom starts with the small decisions. Stop and think for a moment about your purpose in life and the dreams you have about your future. If you don't know specifics, start with something general like, "To grow stronger in my Christian walk." You can (and probably do) have more than one purpose. Write down your purposes here.

_____

_____

_____

_____

_____

_____

_____

_____

Now think about how these purposes will guide your decisions. Commit in your heart to humble yourself as you read the rest of this book. Be courageous enough to face your own rebellious nature in creating loopholes and purposely doing stupid things. Allow yourself to be challenged to learn what it takes to grow into a woman of wisdom.

Are you ready?

"When pride comes, then comes shame; but with the humble is wisdom."

Proverbs 11:2

chapter 2 smart girls get honest

a perfect plan ruined

At 18, Lisa had never had a "real" boyfriend, but she knew in her heart that nothing would sway her from her Godly value of sexual purity. When the time was right for God to bring her future husband into her life, they would walk out their relationship with integrity and character. Maybe they would be in ministry together. Maybe they would start a family and achieve her dream of being a wife and mother. That was her plan. It was a good plan.

How then did this same girl wind up pregnant at the altar at the age of 20, with a young man who would—just two years later—abandon the marriage and their child for an immoral and rebellious lifestyle?

It's a story I've seen over and over again, sadly. Lisa came from a Christian home but had significant gaps in her spiritual development. Her father was a reverent man who provided a steady paycheck, but he was very quiet and kept to himself. Her mother spent her time and money on a secret addiction. Her siblings led lives of destructive habits, or like their father, quietly kept to themselves. Lisa took upon herself a matriarchal role as a young teen, tending to the emotional needs of everyone in the home, not to mention the domestic needs of the home as well.

Lisa had a youth leader at church who poured a lot of truth into her, and most of the time Lisa was receptive to that truth and acted on it. Even when they talked about dating and abstinence, they were seemingly on the same page.

There was one catch. Because of Lisa's sunny and compliant disposition, the leadership in her life elevated her to a place of wisdom that her choices hadn't earned her yet. Lisa had not addressed the deep-rooted spiritual conflicts she had developed growing up. She felt strong morally because her convictions were strong, but after only a few months with a boy who said all the "right" things, she learned that her strength faded in light of her unmet need for love and affection.

Lisa was not spiritually ready to be in a dating relationship with anybody, and although her youth leader tried to warn her in the early stages of the relationship, Lisa politely declined the warning. She was in "love," and this Christian boy seemed to have the thumbs up from everyone else in her life.

spiritual & emotional gaps

Even though the boy Lisa married (and I do mean *boy* – although legally an adult, a 19-year-old male will often lack the maturity to be a husband and father) was deceptive and manipulative in his lure on her heart, Lisa's demise was spelled out in her spiritual and emotional gaps long before he came on the scene. A woman can focus so intently on the "jerk who screwed up her life" that she never addresses her own gaps—the ones that led her to fall head-over-heels for a "jerk" in the first place. As Lisa's life unfolded over the next several years as a single mother, she was forced to confront her gaps and find forgiveness and healing in Christ. Your gaps may be completely different. Here is a laundry list of Lisa's biggies:

gap #1 – Inadequate spiritual covering. Like most young people, Lisa had virtually no accountability and discipleship in her home. Her parents, although well-meaning people, did not deliberately dialogue with her about the things she needed to grow in spiritually. They probably weren't in a spiritual place themselves to even know how to do that. I can relate, since my home was very similar. My youth group and youth leaders provided my only active spiritual covering, and they didn't go home with me every night, so their leadership could only partially cover me.

gap #2 – Emotional neglect. Lisa didn't realize how much emotional affirmation she lacked from her parents until she suddenly had a designated source (the boyfriend) to supplement it. That is a very dangerous scenario for any person to be in. That's why it's so important for your parents to pour pure and Godly affirmation into your life. If you don't get the real thing from your parents, you will likely be in search for a counterfeit, like Lisa and like me, and the enemy will make sure you find one. For Lisa, the loving words and sweet embrace of a seemingly Christian male felt like water being poured on the surface of thirsty desert dirt. She became addicted to the feeling she had when she was around someone who made her feel valuable and loved. That feeling kept her devoted to the relationship, even though she knew it was going places God said were off-limits. Her boyfriend was her drug, and she couldn't seem to get enough.

gap #3 – Inadequate training in life. Lisa's parents were very "hands-off" so she was essentially trying to learn her way through life without much guidance. She did foolish things like sharing financial accounts with her boyfriend, legally tying them together before there was ever a commitment toward marriage. Even though she took a few vocational courses after high school and had a job, she had a lot of idle time on her hands and very few goals for her future. So when a boy appeared on her horizon, she had all the reasons in the world to spend every waking moment with him.

Spiritual and emotional gaps are often handed to us by our upbringing. That's not to blame your parents, or mine for that matter, it's just a fact. It is your parents' job to train you for success in life. Some parents answer that call, and some parents are just trying to figure out life themselves, so children get only the portion they've figured out. Again, I'm not trying to place blame. I'm trying to wake you up to see honestly the deficits you've been handed. Even girls raised by *great* parents are subject to temptation and deceit by the enemy, both of which create canyon-sized gaps in spiritual development. You can't do anything to address your gaps unless you clearly see what they are. God wants those gaps bridged in you, and He is more than capable to build those bridges with you. But it's gonna take some work and commitment on your part.

honest assessment

I have a wonderful pastor who taught me the concept he called "honest assessment." It was a life-changing message for me, not only as a mentor to young women, but personally in my daily walk as a Christian.

Honest assessment is found in Scripture all over the place. "Search me and know my heart; try me, and know my anxieties; And see if there is any wicked way in me and lead me in the way everlasting." (Psalm 139: 23-24, NIV). A beautiful picture of honest assessment

You can't do anything to address your gaps unless you clearly see what they are.

48

is found in the story of the sinful woman who poured perfu..
alabaster flask on Jesus' feet (Luke 7: 36-50). Here was one woman .
knew exactly how screwed up her life was, and exactly what the remedy
was—forgiveness at the feet of Jesus. She wasn't trying to be something she
wasn't, and she was humble enough to go to Jesus in spite of the ridicule she
received from others in order to do what was necessary to show her love for
Him. Her act of anointing Him with perfume and drying His feet with her
hair was a deeply intimate expression, especially in that culture.

How would Lisa's life have played out differently if she had taken
an honest look at where she was really at spiritually? She felt strong;
her leaders thought she was strong, but the reality was that she lacked a
daily devotional life before the Lord to make her strong. She didn't have
intimacy with the Savior in a private setting where she was asking Him
regularly, "Show me what's in me that doesn't bring glory to you." She
wasn't spending time worshipping and ministering to the Lord, finding
her emotional satisfaction in Him alone. Sure, she was a good Christian
girl who went to church and had moral convictions, but those things
cannot take the place of a deep relationship with Jesus through the Holy
Spirit. If that kind of relationship is something you desire but have never
experienced, keep reading. I truly believe that God can and will draw you
deeper to Himself throughout the pages of this book.

humility before honor

The Bible says in Proverbs 15:33, "The reverent and worshipful
fear of the Lord brings instruction in Wisdom, and humility comes before
honor." (AMP) When you care about what God thinks of your choices,
wisdom comes freely. Another amazing verse to live by is 1 Peter 5:6,

"Humble yourselves, therefore, under God's mighty hand, that He may lift you up in due time." (NIV) I have learned, and have often taught my children and those I mentor, if you don't humble yourself willingly, you will be humbled... by life if by nothing else.

The first time I was invited to a baby shower for a teenage mom, I was in emotional turmoil the whole time. This young woman was a Christian, and everyone around her seemed to be just tickled to be throwing a party for her. I was a young adult, so I hadn't experienced this kind of thing before and didn't know how to process what I was feeling. I knew that God loved this girl and wanted her baby to be provided for, yet I felt weird ooh-ing and ahh-ing over every baby outfit she unwrapped. Now that I have a good ten years of learning to give me perspective on the event, I realize why I felt so weird.

The teenage mom we were supposed to be celebrating was still living in rebellion to God sexually with her boyfriend. She was refusing God's blessing by not walking in obedience to His command for sexual purity, yet soliciting the blessings of friends and family out of sheer need for financial support. She was not living in a place of humility where she knowingly identified her supreme need for God and her church to help her. Honor had come *before* humility, instead of humility leading to honor, and that upsets the order of God's Kingdom.

It would have been very different if this girl had become pregnant and had a complete turnaround in her heart, accepting her mistake and vowing to walk out the road to motherhood with reverence to the Lord and His guidelines for her life. How I wish she would have had parents who could have coached her through such a delicate set of circumstances. What if her mom could have helped her begin the party with some words of gratitude and humility, thanking everyone for their grace and forgiveness to come alongside her in this season of repentance and restoration? Sadly, most parents don't even think that way, so how can their children learn to?

Does God want us to come around pregnant teenagers, even when they are in rebellion, to show them His love? Absolutely. But we should be careful not to overlook the greatest point of need in a young woman's life during such a season. She needs a Savior. Long after the diapers and cute outfits are outgrown, the consequences of her choices will remain. The greatest gift we could give a woman like this is the peace found in a restored relationship in Christ. That peace is found on the path of repentance.

I wish I could tell you that the teenager in this story grew up to live an obedient Christian life, despite the challenges of being a young, single mother. Unfortunately, she is now a single mother of two, is no longer in church, and does not seem to be in fellowship with God. It is heartbreaking to realize that her children have no concept of the Lord because their mother has not yet found her way back to Him.

The greatest gift we could give a woman like this is the peace found in a relationship with Christ. That peace is found on the path of repentance.

lies and deception

Underneath every mistake and misstep of a young woman are lies and deception of the enemy. His strategy is as old as humankind; the same strategy he used on Eve in the Garden of Eden, he uses on us daily. "You can be in charge. You don't need God to tell you what to do." It's more subtle in some situations than in others, but that lie is there. If the lie is too blatant for you to believe, some good old-fashioned deception will help you swallow it hook, line, and sinker.

With Lisa's situation, the lie was that she could experience true love outside of God's clearly stated boundaries. However, Lisa was too smart to buy that lie outright, so it was cloaked in deception. The deception went something like this, "You're going to get married anyway, so it's okay to go a little further physically, as long as you don't go all the way. True love doesn't happen every day; why hold back how you feel?" But like all lies and deception, as soon as you're hooked, the circumstances escalate and pretty soon you're dealing with situations you swore you'd never be in. And once you've consented to the first level of deception, it starts to spiral beyond what you ever thought possible.

Like all lies and deception, as soon as you're hooked, the circumstances escalate...

Shelley Lubben, American missionary to the porn industry, and an ex-porn star herself, knows all about how deadly believing those lies can be. She grew up in a pseudo-Christian home but got mixed up in drugs and alcohol as a teenager and eventually found herself homeless in Southern California right after high school graduation. Hungry and full of anger, she relented to prostitution as a means of survival, which led to a very painful downward spiral of slavery in her heart and mind to the vicious lies of the enemy. The first time she tried acting in an amateur pornographic movie, she says she remembers the devil speaking the lie to her heart, "See Shelley, I will make you famous and then everyone will love you." The anger toward those who hadn't loved her and the power of the enemy's lies fueled a rage that promoted her in the adult film industry for years.[3]

Shelley's journey out of the industry happened fairly quickly when she met a man who loved her and married her, but her journey out of the pain that had killed the woman inside was a slow one. She and her husband turned their hearts to God, got in a good church where they heard the truth of the Word to combat the lies, and over eight years saw their hearts and minds transformed by God's healing power.

take a good look

You have a unique opportunity right now to take a good look at the spiritual and emotional gaps in your heart and mind that the enemy wants to exploit for your destruction. If you will ask the Holy Spirit to show you the gaps, He *will*. He might show you through Scripture; He might show you through trusted friends and mentors who see things from an outside perspective; or He might speak to you in a still small voice. He might do all three! God wants you to know the deficiencies you've been handed by your upbringing. He wants you to be honest about the rebellion you've allowed into your own heart, too. Like Eve in the garden, it does you no good to hide from Him. He knows everything you've faced, and He wants to help you out of the pain.

Remember, before honor comes humility. If you want to experience God's hand to lift you up to a place of blessing and destiny, you must humble yourself to see where you're really at. You can't win the race until you actually get to the starting line. You've got to get real before God to get right with him. He's not looking for a super-Christian. He's looking for you. He knows your name, what's in your heart, what you are destined to become, and all it will take to get you there. He knows every hurt or wound that has been inflicted upon you beyond your choosing. Won't you open yourself to Him? Allow yourself to feel the pain and frustration of years spent out of His will, because then you can really embrace the forgiveness He offers.

When Lisa's husband left her and their child, the suffering and emotional trauma she faced was severe. Thankfully, the devastation she experienced brought her to her knees in surrender to God. She realized He was the only way she would be able to survive emotionally, financially, and spiritually. Recognizing that her child needed a mom who was whole, Lisa immersed herself in a healthy Christian community where she was able to address the deep-rooted issues and find healing. It was not an overnight process, and it was not without temptation to go back to her old codependent ways. She had missteps, but she learned the keys of repentance and forgiveness. During her years as a single mom, the Lord led her to go to college, something that in the natural may have seemed impossible at one point. Now, she is a college graduate. Before her child was out of elementary school, the Lord had miraculously brought her a wonderful husband and had restored her dreams, giving her a hope and a future. Her life is now a testimony of God's faithfulness when we will give up our ways for His ways.

What about you? Take a good look at where your life is at spiritually. Have you surrendered your life and your ways to Christ, giving up what you want for what He has instead? Do you know God, or do you know *about* Him? Have you ever thought about how healthy or unhealthy your heart is emotionally? Do you openly acknowledge your emotions to God in prayer, or do you keep emotions from him and everyone else so you can look strong and "together"?

put it into action

God knows exactly where you're at spiritually, and He wants to help you see that reality as well. Pray and ask the Lord to reveal areas of your life where you have gaps. Ask Him for the humility to see yourself clearly and to see which areas in your life need growth. Get with a trusted friend, leader, mentor, or parent (gasp!) and ask them to help you identify areas that need to be addressed in order to move forward and become a woman of wisdom.

Write down some of your areas for growth below as they are revealed to you. Hopefully by the end of our journey together, you will look back on these pages and see you've already made progress in addressing them with humility.

1. _____

2. _____

3. _____

"For whoever finds me (wisdom)
finds life, and obtains favor
from the Lord. But he who sins
against me (wisdom) wrongs his own soul;
all those who hate me love death."

Proverbs 8:35-36

chapter 3
smart girls realize the price

sucked in

Heather and I were born in the same year, thousands of miles apart. Both of us had troubled childhoods, but her story turned tragic fast. Her single dad was a drug addict for the first seven years of her life, often openly using drugs with his friends right there in their home—not exactly the ideal environment for a small child. By age 16, Heather was using cocaine, crack and alcohol, no doubt reaching for anything to fill the emptiness carved away by the neglect of her parents. She left her family in New York around the age of 20 to search for some kind of happiness in San Francisco. One night she found herself at a bar in the famous Haight-Ashbury district, barely old enough to drink legally. A handsome man much older than her bought her a drink, and they began a conversation. His name was Roberto, and she would later find out he was 48 years old. She thought he was fascinating.

Roberto invited Heather home with him that night. With alcohol-impaired judgment, she went. When she arrived at his place, she saw rooms filled with bizarre emblems of some kind of magical worship—a goat's head, a chalice of blood, candles, and tarot cards. He offered to predict her spiritual journey through the tarot cards, and she eagerly agreed. She recalled being "extremely moved" by this experience and all that followed. She had finally found something that seemed meaningful to her, and a man who would love her and take care of her.

But the story doesn't end there. Roberto and Heather moved to Las Vegas a few months later, and Roberto convinced her to apply for a job with Loomis Armored Cars. She actually got an interview and was offered the job. Each morning before she went to work, she willingly let Roberto play a meditation-type hypnosis videotape for her. When the video ended, she would come out of her hypnotic trance, kiss Roberto, and go off to work. Life was good as far as Heather was concerned.

But one morning in the string of a hundred "normal" mornings, Heather's life took a drastic turn, never to be the same again. The day started off the same as every other day, breakfast, getting ready for work, and a hypnosis video. Only when she came out of the hypnotic state on this day, she was immediately confronted by a clearly agitated Roberto giving her specific instructions. She couldn't believe her ears. He wanted her to hijack the armored car she was to drive at work that day, and he followed his directions with a threat: "If you don't do exactly as I say, I will kill you."

Heather believed his threat. By this time in their relationship she knew that he had served over twenty years in prison for killing a guard in an armored car robbery.

This frightened young woman, confused at the sudden turn in Roberto's approach to her, felt like she had nowhere to turn. Mentally vulnerable because of whatever hypnotic messages she had received, not to mention the emotional manipulation by this older and sinister man, and believing her life was in jeopardy, Heather did exactly as she was told that morning.

Within three hours, Heather helped Roberto steal about three million dollars in Las Vegas' most famous heist. Immediately afterward, she was forced by her lover onto a private plane and the two of them were off to an undisclosed location. During the flight, the realization started setting in that Roberto had been planning this crime for months with elaborate detail. He didn't love her at all; he had used her. Her world was shattered as she watched this man whom she thought she loved, whom she said she would have given her life for, turn into a monster.

While I was studying for college mid-terms with friends, Heather was coerced to commit a crime that would change her life forever. All because of a bar she happened to walk into as a young woman, which led to her getting drunk with a man she didn't know, which led to an impaired decision to go home with him that night. What would have happened to Heather if she had used wisdom and made different choices earlier on? Then again, how many other 21-year-olds have done the exact same thing?

coming to her senses

Heather ran from the law with Roberto for years, eventually ending up across the globe in Amsterdam. For nearly two years, she lived a mindless existence, doing whatever Roberto wanted, too afraid of the consequences if that loyalty was violated. When Heather got pregnant with Roberto's child, something inside her began to change. She realized she had to break free from this controlling and maniacal relationship. After her baby boy was born, she summoned the courage to scrape up $1,000 in cash and sneak out one night with her infant son. She never looked back. The next ten years of her life were spent in hiding, with an assumed identity, trying to provide for her child.

Over that decade, Heather had a lot of time to think about what had happened and what *would* happen in the future if she continued to run. Becoming a mom is life-changing for anyone, but I suspect that for Heather motherhood placed an unspoken expectation on her that she desperately wanted to live up to. She wanted to give her son a good life. She must have thought of the crippling effect her parent's bad choices had on her life. How could she do the same thing to her own child? He didn't even have a legal identity or citizenship because she was a fugitive. How would they deal with that in a few years when he wanted to go to college, or get a job, or pay taxes, or get married? The only remedy was heart-wrenching. In order for him to grow up to be a responsible young man she had to own her mistakes, confess her crime, and accept the consequences—no matter what they were.

And that's what she did. One sunny morning, twelve years after her crime, Heather Tallchief flew back to the United States and turned herself in for the robbery she committed. She was sentenced to five years in prison. Her son remained in Europe with her new boyfriend, a man whom she hoped to marry after she served her time.[4] She missed five of her son's birthdays, and by the time her sentence was fulfilled he was 15 years old, already through puberty and most likely seeming more like a man than a boy in many ways. No doubt those five years without his mother taught this young man the power of choices, consequences, and doing what's right no matter what the cost.

the common denominators

U.S. District Judge Philip Pro, the man who sentenced Heather Tallchief to five years in prison, said Heather is all too typical of the female defendants who stand before him every day. Like her, most of them come from backgrounds that include bad childhoods, bad choices and bad boyfriends.

"You created the situation you find yourself in," Pro told Heather in the courtroom that day.

Notice the common denominators the judge observed: bad childhoods, bad choices, and bad boyfriends. While this is not every girl's story, I would have to agree that these three factors are often to blame for the tragic demise of a young woman's destiny. We talked about bad childhoods and the importance of recognizing the gaps in your upbringing in the previous chapter. We'll talk more about boyfriends and the importance of guarding your heart in chapter seven. Let's get down to the nitty gritty of the bad choices and the steep price they bring.

Bad childhoods. Bad choices. Bad boyfriends.

you can't afford that

Did you know there is a war for your destiny happening every day? Whether you are aware of it or not, there is a fierce battle going on for your soul, and the stakes are very high. If you choose to cruise along with the culture, you will most assuredly be led down a path of comfort, convenience, compromise, and ultimately self-destruction. The Bible says, "...wide is the gate and broad is the path that leads to destruction." (Matthew 7:13)

The decisions you make in today's day and age carry far more severe consequences than the decisions of women in previous generations. In the past twenty-five years, the statistics for unmarried women giving birth have more than doubled.[5] Unfortunately, for both baby and mom, sexually irresponsible behavior is behind many of these pregnancies.

How are these women providing for their children? A single mother will be forced to choose one of three paths: work, welfare, or a combination of both. Work is tough unless she is fortunate enough to have completed higher education before giving birth. Let's say you luck out and land a job that pays $13 per hour ($4 more on average than a shift supervisor makes at Starbucks®). That's roughly $1,700 each month, after taxes. The average daycare will take $750 of that monthly income (for one child, not an infant, more or less depending on what state you live in).[6] That leaves a single mom with a little less than $1,000 to pay rent, insurance, utilities, gas, and groceries. That is no easy task. Relying on state aid is not an issue of laziness for many women – it is simply survival.

The health repercussions of a young woman's choices today are also far more serious than those for the previous generations. When I was a teenager, STD's were just beginning to make the news. I mean, we all knew about AIDS, but to our naïve minds, that seemed like a disease that only existed in Africa or highly populated homosexual communities. How has that changed?

A progressive newspaper in Wisconsin reported the following. "All across the country, state public health programs are battling huge increases in STDs. Several decades ago, there were only two common STDs: syphilis and gonorrhea. Today, there are more than twenty-five. The Center for Disease Control (CDC) estimates that there are approximately nineteen million new STD infections each year — almost half of them among young people 15 to 24 years of age. And these reported cases are only a fraction of actual cases, since up to eighty percent of infections have no symptoms and remain undetected, meaning that their victims unknowingly continue to spread them to others."[7]

Aside from financial and health consequences, a teenager raised by a mother who still battles her own failures simply doesn't have the level of training as a teenager raised by a mother who has a clear understanding of who she is in Christ.

That's why it's critical that you identify your areas of needed growth now so you don't repeat the cycle. No matter what kind of upbringing you received, God can and will redeem your life if you will offer everything you are to Him. He is the only one who gives beauty when you hand Him ashes.

God can and will redeem your life if you will offer everything you are to Him.

mayday! mayday!

I sat across from a beautiful, young single mother, one whom I had known for several years, pleading with her not to go through with it. I asked her to wait, just a few months, get counsel, wait on God for a plan. Clearly my plea was too late, the ship of her heart had sailed. The next morning she married someone who she had only spent seven days with. After connecting for two months with him on the phone and email, she was convinced that he was the one God wanted for her. A few days later she packed her and her baby girl's belongings and moved to a new state to start her new life with prince charming. She was just 20 years old.

Within the first year of her marriage, this young mother found herself overwhelmed with the reality of her new life. What should have been a season of newlywed bliss was actually a life of volatile arguments over her new husband's pornography addiction and his temper. Wanting better for her young daughter and a new baby now in her womb (conceived early in her failing marriage), she filed for divorce and moved back home. Another child with a new boyfriend followed a few years later. Today she is a divorced single mother of three, who eventually got right with God and fought her way through college to provide for her children.

She understands the steep price that comes with the consequences of her choices, especially how it affects the next generation.

Obviously marriage is a big deal, one with a lifetime of repercussions—beautiful, tragic, or something in between. That paralyzes some to the point of never marrying. Others seem to race full-steam-ahead, full of emotion and the hope that they will beat the odds. With the divorce rate so high, I often wonder if many reckless marriages occur simply because the two people have been conditioned by our culture to believe that *if* the marriage is found to be a "mistake," it can easily be "undone." To some, divorce is a back-up plan, one that they don't plan on using, but available if necessary. If the bride and groom are Christians, they may never actually give voice to that belief, or even know it's there for that matter. But when so many Christian marriages end in divorce, it's understandable that young people would disregard the permanence of the marriage commitment. God says it's forever, but everything else they observe says the opposite.

God says it's forever, but everything else they observe says the opposite.

In today's day and age, people meet on the internet and skip to the committed relationship stage in a matter of weeks. Some of these are even devoted to the idea of monogamy and Christian values. And while some may end in "happily ever after," many don't. Whether you meet your future spouse in the third grade or on eHarmony,° the stakes are just as high when it comes to committing your life to that man before the Lord. When it comes to life-long decisions like marriage, it's a recipe for disaster if you are just *guessing*. The alternative to that is to develop a life of wisdom before you ever even consider marriage, and to first and foremost know how to obey the voice of the Lord in matters great and small.

the inconsequential

Most people acknowledge the high stakes of big decisions like marriage. But what about the choices that seem "inconsequential," meaning, without consequences? Most people, even Christians, view certain choices as hinging on their own responsibility, and others–the biggies–as ones to get God involved in. It's like they're saying, "Thanks, big guy... I got this one." How does that work when each choice you make leads to bigger and higher-stake choices down the road?

For example, when I was a teenager, I didn't ask God who or if I should date. I asked my *girlfriends*, of course. I wanted to know what they thought of Mr. Hottie-Face. With their approval, I felt totally justified in jumping into relationship after relationship.

So when my senior prom came around and I didn't have a date, I didn't think twice about letting a friend set me up with a boy I didn't even know. Why not? I reasoned that he seemed like a Christian boy (I didn't ask). It's just one date, a little dancing, what could go wrong? Never once did it occur to me to ask God what He thought of the whole idea.

So, I went to prom with someone I barely knew. And that night was the beginning of a relationship that lasted a few years and eventually started steering toward marriage. Not as romantic as it sounds. Those years were the most spiritually confusing years of my life. I knew I was out of God's will; I knew I could not marry this boy as I had promised, but I loved the way he seemed to love me. I had trusted friends speak hard truth to me about the relationship, and I refused to listen. My heart grew further and further away from the Lord as my relationship with this young man grew more intense emotionally and physically. Through it all, I was a wreck. I was convicted at every turn but too afraid to give up and give in to God.

Finally, at my best friend's wedding, I had a miraculous intervention by the Holy Spirit. As I watched the bride and groom pledge their lives to each other for the King and the Kingdom, I realized this type of celebrated and Godly relationship was not in my future because I was disobeying God. I went from that wedding ceremony with the resolve to not throw away God's destiny for me, and to not be part of helping someone else do the same.

In the months that followed, my heart changed radically. I broke off the relationship, as brutal as that felt, and began to hear God speak to me again. I finally felt clear direction from the Lord about things I had been very confused about earlier. God led me to work for a ministry in Oklahoma for my last summer before college graduation, and it was there I eventually met my Jesse (my soul mate and husband).

I remember being in a post office in Tulsa and writing the date at the top of a check—May 4, 1996. Instantly I realized it was the date I had set to marry my previous boyfriend. I burst into tears, right there in the line for my stamps. I knew God had delivered me (and him!) from a disastrous future. Instead of being in a white dress, about to pledge my life to the wrong man...on May 4, 1996, I bought stamps, had an uneventful afternoon, watched a movie, and fell asleep in the apartment I rented by myself with a very clear conscience and a sense of destiny.

Some may say that things all worked out in the long run, so who cares if I was in a wrong relationship for a couple of years? I am convinced that God's perfect will for me was to meet my husband without the baggage

I am convinced that God's perfect will for me was to meet my husband without the baggage I obtained through that long season of disobedience.

I obtained through that long season of disobedience. Although I had fully repented, it would take me five years into my marriage to work through the strongholds that had formed in my mind because of the moral compromises I had allowed myself to make.

So you see, my prom date choice really *did* matter. The small choices you face are just as important as the ones you may classify as "big." All of the choices after the small ones get harder and harder.

making hard choices

Often the hardest choices to make are the ones that carry the most severe consequences. What would you do if you were a 20-years-old waitress and a famous football player came into the restaurant where you worked and started flirting with you? Flattering? Sure. Would you act on it? What would you do if he asked for your phone number? You don't actually know this person, but because you know so much about him as a celebrity, you may feel like you know enough to know he's a good guy. What if you were pretty sure he was married? Would it change your choice?

Most women naturally desire to be pursued and affirmed by the opposite sex, and it takes a lot of courage and maturity to actually *resist* that. I believe that's why God gave us fathers (biological or spiritual) and brothers in Christ. We should find the affirmation from men in healthy relationships where there are boundaries and accountability so we don't have to search for it elsewhere. So what about all the women who don't have those kind of healthy relationships?

Sahel Kazemi was a woman with a troubled childhood. Raised for nine years in Iran, she came to the United States to live with relatives after both of her parents were killed. From age 9 to age 16 she was in

Florida with aunts and uncles, and at 16 she and her boyfriend moved to Nashville, TN. (Okay, number one... don't move anywhere with a boyfriend, especially not at that age!)

Four years went by after Sahel (known as Jenny to her friends) moved to Nashville, and we don't know much about what kind of life she led. We know that by the time she was 20 her relationship with the boyfriend she had been with for so long was over. She worked as a waitress in an upscale hotel, often frequented by Nashville's many celebrities, including Steve McNair, previously the quarterback for the Tennessee Titans.

Sahel caught McNair's eye, and it wasn't long before the two were dating. Wait a minute, isn't McNair married? Doesn't he have children? Star-struck and naïve, Sahel seemed to believe McNair was divorcing his wife and that she would be the next Mrs. McNair. The football player bought her lavish gifts and spoiled her in a way she had always dreamed of.

But somewhere during their relationship Sahel's life started to unravel. Mounting bills on an upscale apartment and two car payments were stressing her out. She started posting her furniture for sale on the Internet just to bring in some money. Then on July 2, 2009, she got arrested for a DUI and sent to jail. She told police she wasn't drunk, just high. McNair, who was with Sahel when she was pulled over, got to go home that night but bailed her out the next morning.

The next detail of the story is chilling. The following day, the evening of July 3, during her shift at the restaurant, Sahel snuck out to the parking lot to buy a gun for $100. The next night, July 4, she left work early and headed to the condo she often stayed at with McNair, obviously a second residence for him.

McNair wasn't home when she got there and was reportedly seen bar-hopping in Nashville (again, where are the wife and kids?). He finally returned to the condo late. The next day his best friend of twenty years found two dead bodies in the condo. Steve McNair had been murdered with four shots, one directly to the temple. Sahel Kazemi lay near him with a single shot to her temple. The police ruled that she committed suicide after killing her famous football player boyfriend.

According to an article in *The Tennessean*, friends said Sahel had begun to suspect McNair was seeing someone else and had realized the divorce she had hoped for was basically a fantasy. The weight of humiliation, rejection, and abandonment seemed too much for her to bear. She apparently saw no way out of the emotional prison she was facing except to end everything permanently. [8]

What can we learn from Sahel Kazemi? She was definitely a woman with a lot of deficits and gaps in her upbringing, no doubt traumatized by the events that left her orphaned. She probably felt as if she was on her own and needed to set her own course for happiness, so moving to Tennessee with her boyfriend must have made sense to her. And when a fast-track to happiness came along in the form of a rich and famous boyfriend, she probably saw it as a huge break.

But let's keep in mind that this girl was not living her life with the paradigm of a Christian. Sahel did not look to the truth of Scripture for guidance. She did not have the Holy Spirit to turn to for peace and comfort, helping her cope with difficult emotions and decisions. Her choices probably make sense to most young women in America. But her choices ended tragically, and even though she couldn't see a viable alternative at that point, it did exist. She could have made a different choice. She could have stood up for her own value and said, "Obviously this is not turning out to be what I hoped it would. I'm going to move on. Nice knowin' ya, Steve." She could have sold her fancy car and moved into a less expensive apartment. She could have moved away and started over for that matter. But it would have required her to humble herself and face those who she had impressed with her grand celebrity stories. And that seemed to be too high of a price for her. So she ended her own life, took away another woman's husband and the father of four children. Other people wound up paying the price that Sahel refused to pay herself.

put into action

By this point in your life, you have no doubt seen some pretty tough circumstances that have come from poor choices, either by your own doing or in another's life. What price is too high to pay? It's amazing to me the lasting consequences young girls will suffer just to feel the temporary affection from another person who will in no way be part of their future. Think about the price tags you've seen for stupidity. Write a few down as a reminder of the unfortunate realities stupidity can bring. (NOTE: Please be sure not to step into the sin of judgment over other people's sin. Just list the choice and the obvious hard consequences that came as a result).

1. _____
   _____

2. _____
   _____

3. _____
   _____

Now think about some prices that you *haven't* had to pay at this point in your life, but that you know would be devastating. These are consequences to keep before you as you build your future with the Lord.

3: smart girls realize the price

They serve as a warning to deter you from a life of foolishness. For example, you might think of suffering a broken heart, having to confess to your parents something shameful, or even going to jail.

1. _____

_____

2. _____

_____

3. _____

_____

"The fear of the LORD is the
beginning of wisdom; A good
understanding have all those who do
His commandments. His praise
endures forever."

Psalm 111:10

chapter 4 smart girls fear the Lord

sinning against the Lord

Sophie was a pastor's daughter who grew up knowing all the right and spiritual things to say. She was on the worship team at church. She was class president at school, a leader on her basketball team, and seemed to have everything going for her. Imagine her parents' surprise when they got a phone call from the police saying she had been ticketed for driving under the influence at the age of 17 and was being held at the police station until her parents could come pick her up.

Sophie had started drinking about a year prior, partially because her social circle was broadening to include kids who partied and drank, opening up more opportunity for her to join them; and partially because she enjoyed the "freedom" she said she felt after she had a few drinks in her. She admitted that being a pastor's daughter felt at times like the whole world was watching her, and she found she could escape that perceived pressure when she got drunk.

The night Sophie got her DUI, everything she had been afraid of came crashing down on her. She had hidden her lifestyle from her parents, her youth pastor and the teachers and coaches at her Christian school. When the jig was up, there was no more hiding. Everyone knew. She lost every privilege imaginable at home. She had to write a letter to her principal asking for forgiveness for violating the school's honor code. She had to step down from the worship team and the basketball team, and the whispers of her classmates caused her to feel ashamed. Sophie was devastated.

In the midst of the gossip and the consequences, Sophie did something that completely changed the outcome of her situation. A few weeks after her arrest, she ran to the Lord, fully repenting for her sinful actions and rededicating her life to Him completely. The change in her life was immediately evident.

Sophie testified before her peers almost a year later at youth camp. She explained the turning point for her was when she realized that even more important than breaking the rules of her parents, and the law, was the fact that she had sinned against the Lord. For an entire year she had been running from the conviction of the Holy Spirit and deliberately disobeying His instruction to confess her sin and turn from her ways. The words of Psalm 51:4-6 penetrated her.

"You're the One I've violated, and you've seen it all, seen the full extent of my evil. You have all the facts before you; whatever you decide about me is fair. I've been out of step with you for a long time, in the wrong since before I was born. What you're after is truth from the inside out. Enter me, then; conceive a new, true life." (MSG) Sophie realized that despite being born into a godly family, she was not made right with God because of her parents' faith. And she was not made right by doing well in school or in sports. She had to choose to live for God herself, wholeheartedly, not halfway.

What you're after is truth from the inside out.

What Sophie learned that year was the fear of the Lord. And the Bible says the fear of the Lord is the beginning of wisdom (Psalm 111:10).

the right kind of fear

The fear of the Lord sounded like a really strange and scary concept when I was growing up. Even after I accepted Christ, I did not fully understand the terminology. Am I supposed to be afraid of God? I thought God was love. I was deeply confused, which was a huge contributing factor to my profound stupidity. I was trying to follow "rules" that I thought made me a better Christian (don't drink, don't do drugs, don't have sex). But I did a lot of other stuff that I didn't want to acknowledge, and it was all sin against the Lord. Much later in life I learned that my disobedience to the Lord and unconfessed sin actually damaged my relationship with Him. I worried a lot about what others thought of me for a long time, but I didn't really think about what the *Lord* thought of me. In fact, I never really inquired what He thought of my choices and attitudes at all. I was doing my Christian thing, totally under the radar, or so I thought. But all along, God was watching me and waiting for me to acknowledge that I had dishonored His place of Lordship and disrespected Him.

To fear the Lord means to be in awe of Him, to respect Him, and to give reverence to His holiness. Perhaps because I didn't grow up with a father, and my mother was pretty weak on the leadership and discipline side, I just didn't even understand the kind of respect God deserved.

The fear of the Lord has to do with our attitude in obedience to Him. Obviously any form of disobedience also shows disrespect. When we continually disobey God, we are dismissing the implications of our sin and how it affects our relationship. I can't experience intimacy and truly deep relationship with Him when I am dismissive or casual about my disobedience. I am still His child, but our relationship is strained, and it remains strained until I repent. When my relationship with God is out of harmony, I am unable to fully experience the blessing and intimacy that is supposed to be part of my Christian walk. As a loving and just parent, my heavenly Father will withhold blessing until I come to Him with a softened heart that is ready to get right. Repentance reveals that my attitude has returned to properly reverencing and respecting His Lordship. In effect, repentance says, "You were right, Lord. I was not."

When my children are corrected or disciplined for something they did wrong, they will occasionally refuse to apologize out of pride. Many car rides have been spent in silence because they do not want to say what needs to be said to make things right. Often, after a few minutes of silence, they will try to bring up some casual topic of conversation as if I've forgotten what just happened. I feel disrespected if my son changes the subject from the lie he just told to the party he's excited about going to. The fact of the matter is, until my son repents, our relationship feels scratchy.

It can be the same way with God. He patiently and lovingly will bring us back to the sin issue. Sure, we can just go on and pretend like nothing happened. We can change the subject to avoid the intimacy that produces repentance, but we will not feel complete peace in our relationship with Him until we deal with it. I've had times in my life where I have finally come to God to repent, and I hear Him whisper to my heart, "I've been waiting for you." I humbly offer Him His rightful place of Lordship and adjust my attitude to honor Him again.

Fearing the Lord means we put obedience to Him before anything else in our lives. In the book of Exodus, Pharaoh ordered midwives to kill all baby boys born to Hebrew women. I love what it says in Exodus 1:17, "But the midwives feared God and did not do as the king of Egypt commanded them." (NLT) A note in my *Spirit-Filled Life Bible* states, "The fear of the Lord produces wise, healthy actions, as in the present reference: the midwives were more afraid of angering God by destroying innocent babies than they were afraid of disobeying Pharaoh." [9]

Obedience to God teaches us what we need to know for wise living. If you want to be teachable, fear the Lord. Psalm 25:14 says, "The secret of the Lord is with those who fear Him, and He will show them His covenant." Those who are close to God get to learn His secrets, the things He discloses to those He can trust. When you reverence, awe, and respect God, He knows He can trust you.

When you have access to God's secrets—when He knows He can trust you, you will make good choices and stay on solid ground.

you don't need your eye

Jesus said, "If your right eye causes you to sin, pluck it out and cast it from you; for it is more profitable for you that one of your members perish, than for your whole body to be cast into hell." (Matthew 5:29)

Now that got me to thinking one day. I was talking to my son about the lengths God expects us to go to so we can eradicate sin from our lives, and this Scripture came to mind. Plucking your eye out is pretty radical. And gross. And, well, hard to explain to others. Think about it. "What happened to you?" they ask. "Well," you say, "I kept looking at pornography, so I decided to gouge out my eye to help me live clean."

If something in your life is causing you to sin, the only reasonable solution for you to be free is to do something radical. Most women are completely unwilling to do that. I remember confronting a young woman about spending time with people who she knew were bad influences, enticing her to dabble with pot and alcohol. This wasn't some degenerate who just couldn't get clean. This was a college student with a call on her life who had been free from addictions in her past for some time. I told her she was putting her future in jeopardy, not just the "destiny" part, but her relationship with the Lord. I asked her point blank if she was willing to give up her so-called "friendships" in order to get free. She lowered her eyes in shame and shrugged. (That's a "no," by the way.) My first thought was, "Have you no fear of the Lord?" I didn't even ask the question. The answer was obvious.

If you fear the Lord and care about pleasing Him more than pleasing yourself or others, you'll love obedience and right-living more than your own comfort. Do you need your eyes to live? No, you don't. Living with one eye would be uncomfortable and probably a little embarrassing at times, but it would be worth the discomfort and embarrassment if it kept you from throwing your relationship with God away. Jesus is bringing that point home. He's not seriously encouraging you to mutilate yourself, He's provoking you to evaluate your attitude toward obeying God. Do you love your sin more than you love God? Are you willing to give up anything in order to be right with God?

Do you fear the Lord?

temptation's antidote

The fear of the Lord will keep you from falling to temptation. When you fear the Lord, you are consistently concerned with what obedience to the Lord looks like in any situation, which helps you evaluate what would honor God most.

Some decisions in life will be harder to make than others because they pull on your emotions with tempting (and faulty) solutions. For example, look at the temptation to live beyond what you can afford. It's not uncommon for an 18 or 19-year-old to receive a credit card application in the mail. They're handed out with candy bars and cash on college campuses around the nation. Once you get your first credit card, and you have that purchasing power in your hand, it's hard not to buy that cute sweater in the store window—after all, it's half price! The temptation to buy something you don't have the money for will wage war against your ability to make a wise decision. No matter how seemingly "small" the challenge is—whether it's sweater temptation, chocolate temptation, or back-seat-of-your-boyfriend's-car temptation—it's something that you need to be prepared to fight against.

I think we've given the word "temptation" such a negative spin that we tend to forget all of us deal with it, and we may as well be honest about it! There is not one person on this earth who hasn't been tempted—even Jesus was. You haven't sinned because you've been tempted; you've sinned when you've acted on that temptation. And in order to make good decisions in the face of strong temptation, we have to know how to deal with temptation scripturally.

You haven't sinned because you've been tempted; you've sinned when you've acted on that temptation.

When it comes to temptation, the devil is really good at what he does. He doesn't play fair, that's for sure. The story of Jesus being tempted in Luke 4:1-13 is a great example. Here He was, denying His flesh by fasting in the desert for forty days, doing all the right things and not straying into sin in any way. And still—boom—temptation came. The devil knew Jesus was starving from forty days without food, so he tempted Him to turn a stone into bread. He also tempted Him with dominion over the kingdoms of the world, and with a challenge over His Lordship ("If you are the Son of God…"). In the face of each temptation, Jesus responded with a profound and simple answer. He simply quoted Scripture—the truth—by saying, "It is written." Do you think that response might work for us as well?

When Katie graduated from college, her life was a mess. Although she had given her life to the Lord as a child, the emotional abuse she had suffered from her father was severe, and it plunged her into six years of bondage to sexual sin to numb the pain. She had even gone so far as to have an affair with a married man. In the midst of the darkest season of her life, there was a moment of clarity where she saw her sin and heard God speak to her about leaving everything behind to move back home so she could begin to heal spiritually.

When Katie got home, she pursued God like never before. She could feel herself gaining strength to battle the sexual temptation she had felt so strongly before. One key verse God gave her in that season was Proverbs 4:23, which says, "Guard your heart above all else, for it determines the course of your life." (NLT) Katie had to rely on that Scripture over and over. When the really cute guy from Bible study sat next to her, she had to say it quietly to herself! That Scripture from the Lord was truth, the very key she needed to overcome temptation. (And by the way, that cute guy from Bible study became her husband years later!)

nothing but the truth

The only way to expose the lies of the devil is with the truth. Remember the Scripture about the person who fears the Lord knowing God's secrets and being shown His commandments? That means you will know His truth! If you know the truth, speak the truth, and act on the truth of the Word, you can withstand temptation to make wise and Godly decisions. You can not be prepared to handle temptation if you do not know the truth of God's Word for your situation. Where self-control runs out, truth will always remain.

You can't avoid temptation entirely because it's a part of life, but you can use wisdom to stay away from situations that are especially tempting. I love how Dr. Wanda Turner, a passionate preacher, puts it, "The devil knows what kind of cheese you like, and underneath that cheese is a trap to kill you." You might think that you have the willpower to stand against a certain temptation in your life, and so you'll flirt with danger by brushing right up against it. The ridiculous sense of security you have is really pride and could very well be the cheese the devil purposely put on your trap. You're enjoying a delicious bite of cheese one moment, and the next moment you're caught in a painful metal apparatus!

The apostle Paul brings a warning in Romans 12:3. "Don't think you are better than you really are. Be honest in your evaluation of yourselves, measuring yourselves by the faith God has given us." (NLT) If you know what your particular cheese is—even if you just have a hunch—stay away from anything that remotely looks, smells, or tastes like that cheese.

Remember, you're up against an enemy who does not play fair. He knows your weaknesses better than you do! Most teenagers who wind up in drug addiction can trace their lost battle back to a certain piece of cheese— usually the desire to be accepted and "admired" for trying something, or the desire to medicate pain in their family life. Young adults who are living with huge amounts of debt can trace their lost battle back to a certain piece of cheese—usually the desire to impress others with material things, or the faulty coping mechanism of spending money to make themselves feel better.

A 17-year-old single mother will tell you her cheese was a good-looking boy who told her things she was dying to hear. Some of the cheeses in your life you may be able to identify, but many of them you will not.

know your weaknesses

So how do you stay away from cheese on a trap if you have no idea what your cheese is? All of us have weaknesses that we're blind to, to some degree. We talked about how to uncover your gaps in chapter two, and the same principles apply. If you are a Christian, you have the Holy Spirit to help you uncover the blind areas of your life. However, these things can be uncovered and never dealt with because of pride. Like I said before, it's painful to be humble enough to admit where you are weak. Once you discover the areas where you're weak, you need to stay as far from that cheese as possible! Someone who has a problem with lust, for example, will need to be extremely careful about watching movies and television shows that have even the mildest form of sensuality. If you struggle with irresponsibility with money, ask someone to help keep you accountable with your budget until you've grown in that area. If you find yourself smoking pot every time you go to the skate park, then I suggest you skate somewhere else. It's not hard to figure out, but it is hard to practice. (Here's another hint: I bet if you asked your parents and/or adult leaders in your life what your cheese might be, they could probably tell you in a heartbeat).

I bet if you asked your parents and/or adult leaders in your life what your cheese might be, they could probably tell you in a heartbeat.

the nature of deception

Temptation often starts with a subtle and deadly trick by the enemy called deception. *Webster's Dictionary* defines deception this way: "To lead another into error, danger, or a disadvantageous position by underhanded means. Deception involves the deliberate misrepresentation of the truth."

Years ago I watched a couple of Christian illusionists astonish a mostly-teenage crowd at a youth event. They randomly selected two kids from the audience of over five thousand to participate in their next trick. One kid thumbed through a giant business phone book until the other one yelled, "Stop!" forcing the first kid to randomly choose a phone number from the book. Then the illusionists had the kids sit down as they revealed a giant table with the exact phone number just chosen taped to the top of it. They had successfully deceived the crowd. We had missed something for sure! How could they have known the phone number in order to get the table ready for the trick? How could they have planned when the kid would yell, "Stop!" to choose the phone number in the first place?

The illusionists were making a very valuable point that is timeless in its application: deception only works when the person or people it's aimed at have no idea it's happening. Some people think, "Well, if I was being deceived, I would know." Hardly! That's the whole problem. When you are being deceived, you have no idea!

self-deception

The Bible has a lot to say about deception. And if you are going to avoid deception, you'd better know what God says about how it works.

One lesson to learn that is of utmost importance is the notion of how we deceive *ourselves*. Did you know you could do that? You thought it was all the devil's fault, didn't you? Well, when you do things in cooperation with him rather than in cooperation with the Holy Spirit, you will find yourself picking up on his kind of tricks. Let's look at some Biblical truth (you can also find this information in the book *Victory Over the Darkness*):[8]

1. **You deceive yourself when you say that you have no sin.** If you think you've got it all together, look out! Pride is sin. Pride brings deception and causes you to be vulnerable to temptations that you're not prepared to handle. Galatians 6:3 says, "For if anyone thinks himself to be something, when he is nothing, he deceives himself." 1 John 1:8 says, "If we say that we have no sin, we deceive ourselves, and the truth is not in us."

2. **You deceive yourself when you don't control the words you use.** Our mouths reveal what's in our heart. If you use polluted and disrespectful words in order to fit in or get attention, you are walking on dangerous ground. A woman who speaks a certain way out of a desire to impress others will eventually do ungodly things out of that same desire. James 1:26 says, "If anyone among you thinks he is religious, and does not bridle his tongue but deceives his own heart, this one's religion is useless."

3. **You deceive yourself when you think hanging around immoral and ungodly influences will have no effect on you.** That doesn't mean that as a Christian you should only hang around other Christians. Jesus did call us to be salt and light in the world. But if you primarily spend time with people who do not uphold Biblical truth as the standard for their lives, you will be negatively affected by it, especially

if your personal fellowship with God is infrequent. 1 Corinthians 15:33 says, "Don't be fooled by those who say such things, for bad company corrupts good character." (NLT)

4. **You deceive yourself when you think you can engage in ungodly behavior without enduring negative consequences.** There is a spiritual principle called "sowing and reaping." You may have heard it said, "You reap what you sow." If you don't do your schoolwork, you will flunk. If you disrespect others, you won't have friends. If you cheat, you will be caught. If you play with fire, you will be burned. Galatians 6:7,8 says, "Do not be deceived, God is not mocked; for whatever a man sows, that he will also reap. For he who sows to his flesh will of the flesh reap corruption, but he who sows to the Spirit will of the Spirit reap everlasting life."

5. **You deceive yourself when you hear the Word but do not practice it.** Knowing the truth and choosing not to act on it (or being lazy enough to put it off) makes you extremely vulnerable to the enemy. James 1:22-25 says, "Be doers of the word and not hearers only, deceiving yourselves. For if anyone is a hearer of the word and not a doer, he is like a man observing his natural face in a mirror; for he observes himself, goes away, and immediately forgets what kind of man he was."

6. **You deceive yourself when you practice sexual sin.** The Bible says that all other sin is outside of the body, but sexual sin is against your own body. Sexual sin and lust create a false line of reasoning in your own mind to justify pleasure at any cost. You cannot remotely make wise choices regarding a relationship when you're engaging in sexual sin. Even lust, pornography, and masturbation, although some may see them as harmless because they "don't affect others" can severely damage

your conscience about what is right and wrong considering God's sexual boundaries. And when those boundaries get blurred, nothing good can result. James 1:14-16 says, "But each one is tempted when he is drawn away by his own desires and enticed. Then, when desire has conceived, it gives birth to sin; and sin, when it is full-grown, brings forth death. Do not be deceived, my beloved brethren."

All of these areas of self-deception show a lack of fear of the Lord. He has clearly spelled these things out in Scripture, and as Christians we should be growing in the knowledge of the truth so that we can obey Him fully. You might be ignorant to what the Word says about self-deception at the beginning of your Christian walk, but let's get smart and educate ourselves with the knowledge of what God wants to teach us. Ignorance can take you out. He has given us His Word so we will know how to obey Him and live a life that is pleasing to Him.

deceived by others

Besides self-deception, there are other ways that you can be deceived by others and by wicked spiritual influences. Let's look at some of the common ones.

1. **You can be deceived by empty, smooth, and flattering words.** When a 17-year-old boy tells you he loves you, beware! Those words are empty until he is willing to sacrifice and pay the price of waiting for a committed God-kind of love. Other examples of empty words are those of acceptance over peer-pressure issues like, "everybody's doing it." Ephesians 5:6 says, " Let no one deceive you with empty words, for because of these things the wrath of God comes upon the sons of disobedience."

2. **You can be deceived by false signs and wonders.** This includes non-Christian influences that some people consider socially acceptable. Take, for example, horoscopes and zodiac signs. If as a Christian you give weight to these things, you are essentially stripping God of His rightful place in your life as the only One worth trusting for your destiny. It also means you must confront beliefs in your heart that run counter to Scripture such as thinking something is "a sign" that you're on the right path if favorable circumstances seem to come your way (versus praying about the direction you're supposed to take). Mark 13:22 says, "For false christs and false prophets will rise and show signs and wonders to deceive, if possible, even the elect."

3. **You can be deceived by those who say they believe one way, but live another way.** There are many people who say they are Christians, but live in a way that would make their life indistinguishable from an unbeliever. Author and pastor Craig Groeschel puts it this way in his book, *The Christian Atheist:* "Believing in God but living as if He doesn't exist." I've met many people like that over the years. [10] That's why 2 Timothy 3:13 warns about the deception of imposters!

put into action

There's no way you can fear the Lord unless you have truly begun a relationship with Him. Why would you want to obey someone you didn't even know? When you start a relationship with God through accepting the sacrifice of Jesus as payment for your sin, you begin to understand His love for you and His desire to see you live above the temptations of the world and the enemy. If you haven't begun with that first step of repentance and belief in Christ, read more on page 184.

Lets evaluate the areas of deception and temptation that the Holy Spirit illuminated to you as you read this chapter. What common temptations do you face? List them here:

1. _____

2. _____

3. _____

4. _____

What principles of self-deception or deception from others do you see at work in the temptations you just listed?

1. _____

2. _____

3. _____

4. _____

James 1:12 says, "Blessed is the man who endures temptation; for when he has been approved, he will receive the crown of life which the Lord has promised to those who love Him."

Knowing your weaknesses is the first step in gaining strength. I encourage you to look though the lists you just made, making a point to pray about each item. Choose to repent (turn and forsake) temptations and ask the Holy Spirit to help you in every area as you move forward. "For we do not have a High Priest who cannot sympathize with our weaknesses, but was in all points tempted as we are, yet without sin. Let us therefore come boldly to the throne of grace, that we may obtain mercy and find grace to help in time of need." (Hebrews 4:15-16) Also, talk to others who are more mature in their faith and give them permission to observe your life and help you stay accountable (we'll talk more about this in chapter eight).

"This means that anyone who belongs to Christ has become a new person. The old life is gone; a new life has begun!"

2 Corinthians 5:17

chapter 5 smart girls know who they are

you don't know what I've done

I met Melanie at church shortly after I moved to Nashville. She was new in town as well and had just moved there a few months after college graduation. I was taken with her right from the beginning. She was one of the most beautiful young women I had ever met, with high cheekbones and perfect skin. She wore her hair short, which flattered her piercing eyes and heart-shaped face. She was stylishly dressed and fit the part exquisitely for someone who worked at a cosmetics counter in an upscale department store. She had an infectious laugh, and I liked her instantly.

As we began our friendship, certain topics of conversation would come up, and I'd notice her becoming quiet and withdrawn. Sensing a wall in the way we related to one another, I asked her about it one day. It seemed Melanie had a hard time believing she was loveable, by God or anyone else. Likeable? Maybe. But loveable was a different story. She fought tears, avoided eye contact, and told me, "You don't know what I've done."

That seemed strange to me. After all, I'd known women who had been rescued from some pretty crazy stuff—prison, prostitution, eating disorders and drug addiction, just to name a few. I didn't think she could shock me with her story, but she insisted that she wasn't ready to talk about it.

Our friendship changed a bit over the next few years as she entered an intense student intern program at our church and as I stayed at home as a new mom. I didn't mind that our relationship looked different. I watched her from a distance and could tell that God was working on her. She had strong women pouring into her, and she seemed to be blossoming as God brought healing to her life.

Then one day at a small seminar I attended, I was pleasantly surprised to see that Melanie would be sharing her testimony during one of our sessions. At long last I learned what Melanie had been so painfully burying. When she was in high school she had gotten pregnant, and she had chosen to get an abortion. What was amazing was watching this young woman share her story with mostly strangers, and to see that she was finally in a place of healing and redemption from the pain.

For years Melanie had seen herself through the lens of that mistake and the addictions that followed. Even though she was a Christian during those years, she had opened the door to lies about her value and worth. She searched for significance in relationships with men, control over her body image, and substance abuse, only to find that these things heaped more shame and hurt on her already wounded heart. Melanie did not know who she really was back then.

Thankfully, Melanie had finally started to believe the truth about what God thought of her and who she was in Christ. These things helped her appropriately deal with the pain of her abortion and allowed her to experience God's love and forgiveness as she grew spiritually. The Lord brought her an amazing husband, and she has begun the glorious task of teaching her own children to know the Lord. What a testimony. What redemption!

who are you?

When people ask you the question, "Who are you?" you probably naturally answer it first with giving them your name. Is that who you are? Some people change their names legally for one reason or another; does that change who they are? I knew a girl in school whose name was Ann, but in college she changed it to Addison. Perhaps she thought that Ann was too common or plain, and Addison sounded more unique and memorable. But who she was on the inside didn't change when her name better matched her own perception of herself.

As an adult, when I board a plane and sit next to total strangers, one of the first questions that is asked is "What do you do?" meaning, "How are you employed?" It's a way for strangers to gain context about each other and discover common ground to make small talk. Sometimes I reply, "I'm a wife and mother." Sometimes, "I'm a writer." But truthfully, neither of those things really describe who I am. Because as a Christian, who I am in Christ is the only *real* me. It is the determining factor for what I do. The things I do are determined only by the roles God has given me because of who I am in Him. I can't do anything He hasn't given me grace or gifts to do.

As a Christian who I am in Christ is the only real me.

Ask yourself, is who you are determined by what you do, or is what you do determined by who you are? Neil Anderson, founder of Freedom in Christ Ministries, asks this question in his book, *Victory Over the Darkness*. He states, "Your understanding of who God is and who you are in relationship to Him is the critical foundation for your belief system and your behavior patterns as a Christian." [11]

a second chance

Some people go to church their whole life but still don't know what it means to be in Christ, or what it means to be all God created them to be. Kristen Anderson was a teenager like that. She was smart and popular, had a great family, and grew up in church. But when tragedy came her way as a 17-year-old through several deaths of friends and also the death of her grandmother, Kristen found herself depressed and hopeless, without any understanding that God would help her through the pain.

Kristen snuck out of her home one night to hang out with a friend, and on her way back home, a sudden and truly demonic thought entered her mind. As she approached a set of train tracks near her house, with the sound of an approaching engine ringing out in the night, she envisioned ending her life by getting in front of that train. She said she just wanted her emotional pain to end. Impulsively, she lay down on the tracks as the sound of the locomotive drew nearer. With more weight and wind than she could have imagined, the train passed over her, thirty-three freight cars... and then it stopped. Kristen wasn't sure if she was dead or alive, but when she opened her eyes and looked around, she saw her own legs laying behind her about ten feet away. The train had severed her legs, but she was still alive.

Obviously, that event was the beginning of a whole new level of pain for Kristen. Talk about life-changing. The story is gruesome, but it does have a happy ending. God used other Christians to help Kristen understand His love for her in her recovery and to see that He saved her life that night. In an interview with "The 700 Club," Kristen said, "I came to the understanding that I would have been sent to hell if I died. So I realized at that moment that God had given me a second chance to go to heaven and spend eternity with Him."[11] What a merciful God.

Today, Kristen speaks as a confident, godly young woman. She does not have legs, but she has Christ, and her countenance radiates His life. She started *Reaching You Ministries* and is using her life to bring hope to others who are battling depression and suicidal thoughts.

Before her suicide attempt, Kristen did not know who she was meant to be, and was willing to lose it all because it didn't seem worth having. Today she knows the forgiveness of God, who He has called her to be, and the security and peace found through a relationship with Him. Far from her former self, she is not floundering in depression, doubt, and anxiety. She has flourished like a plant finally rooted in healthy soil. She is in Christ, and she's living that way.

simple math

Many young women, even those who have been raised in Christian homes, get lost as they search for significance and value. The prevailing cultural philosophy offers many alluring, yet completely false equations about what makes a person happy and whole, such as:

- beauty + intelligence = happiness
- monetary wealth + status = success
- a great personality + an attractive appearance = doors of opportunity

As women, we see these false equations so often we don't notice how completely we've believed the lies behind them. Have you ever thought to yourself, "If only my family had more money, then my life would be happier." Or, "If only I could lose ten pounds, then I'd feel attractive." We've all gone there from time to time, but too many women stay there. They live their lives thinking, "If only, if only, if only." What a sucky way to live!

Maurice Wagner sums it up in his book, *The Sensation of Being Somebody*, "Try as we might by our appearance, performance, or social status to find self-verification for a sense of being somebody, we always come short of satisfaction. Whatever pinnacle of self-identity we achieve soon crumbles under the pressure of hostile rejection or criticism, introspection or guilt, fear or anxiety. We cannot do anything to qualify for the by-product of being loved unconditionally and voluntarily."[13] Basically, no matter how hard you try to make yourself happy (or even if you think you are happy) through artificial means, it will all soon come tumbling down because only God's kind of love gives you lasting fulfillment.

God's math is simple: you + God = wholeness and meaning.

This world is full of people who seem to have everything but destroy their own lives because the "everything" they seem to have is hollow .

So what does all this have to do with making good choices and learning wisdom as a young woman? A lot of women screw up their lives by making wrong choices on the search for significance in the wrong places. For example, if you are under the impression that you need to be in a romantic relationship in order to feel loved and accepted, then you'll find yourself constantly floating in and out of relationships (or wishing you could). That's a pretty painful way to live, and if that's you, then brace yourself for impact because there's a world of hurt awaiting you. However, when you've settled your search at the foot of the cross, knowing that only the love and acceptance of Christ can complete you, you won't be on a desperate search to pair up, hook up, or otherwise. When you realize the value you have in Christ, you won't be looking to false sources for your worth.

an invitation

If you truly believe that you are precious to the Lord, your choices and behavior will prove it. Too many young women, especially Christian women, have memorized sayings and Scriptures about their value to God, but very few of them live their lives as if they believed it.

I heard a great analogy from a pastor friend one day. If the President of the United States passed a measure pardoning all violations of prostitution, many women who are caught in this lifestyle would breathe a sigh of relief. No more sneaking around. No more worrying about getting "busted" and having her kids taken away from her. But how many women would leave prostitution after the pardon?

What if the President extended an invitation to one of those women to become his bride and sit at his side in the White House as the First Lady? How would that woman's sense of value shift? Think about it: the affection of an attentive man and world leader; a new wardrobe; a beautiful home to live in; and the respect and affirmation of powerful people, decision-makers, and staff members (all extremely intelligent people). Those circumstances would change her forever. She would no longer have a lower view of herself, but would begin to understand her value simply by her new position in life.

Like the former prostitute, you and I have value that is determined by our position. Only it's not a position of honor or success by the world's standards. It's a position determined by just one thing—being in Christ. You're either in Him or you're not.

You are not in Christ because you were born in America where the majority of people would say they believe in God. You are not in Christ because your parents took you to church. You are not in Christ because you go to a Christian school. You are in Christ if—and only if—you have repented of your sinful ways, asked Christ to be Lord of your life, and if you accept and believe that His sacrifice on the cross paid the penalty for all your sin.

...An invitation to come into His chamber, to sit at His table, to be close and intimate with Him.

But being in Christ doesn't stop there—it's not just a pardon from the former life of bondage. It's an invitation to come into His chamber, to sit at His table, to be close and intimate with Him. It's an invitation to be His bride, to know His heart, and understand His ways. Once a woman understands the position He's already given her, her choices and behavior begin to look less and less like the prostitute and more and more like the First Lady. That's the kind of value He's placed on you.

full or empty

If you are in Christ, and your belief system is centered on your value in Him, you will be able to look to Him alone to find your security, significance, and acceptance. When a young woman knows who she is in Christ, she will be compelled to act and make choices according to the reality of her identity. However, when she looks to popular culture or her peer group for her identity, she will find herself making poor decisions based on the inadequacy of that belief system.

The search for security, significance, and acceptance outside of Christ leaves you empty. Now how is an empty woman going to make good decisions? She can't. Empty women make choices in an effort to fill themselves up. However, women who are already full in Christ make choices that keep them on the path and plan He has for them. As a pastor and spiritual father once taught me, "You can't do business out of an empty wagon."

Believe me, being in Christ doesn't mean you are perfect and you never screw up. The great thing about God (well, there are many, but one thing that I love) is that His love toward us never fails, even when we blow it.

Neil Anderson paints it very clearly in the book, *Victory Over the Darkness*. When we disobeyed our parents as children, we experienced negative consequences and (hopefully) discipline. Our disobedient behavior changed the harmony of our relationship with them, but it didn't change the fact that they were still our parents.

In the same way, when we disobey God and do something really dumb, we feel the disharmony in our relationship with Him. But does it change the fact that He is still our Heavenly Father? No! Our position *in Him* doesn't change. We are not made righteous by our own actions; rather, we are covered by the righteousness that Jesus purchased for us when He went to the cross. What makes us Christians is that we accept His righteous payment. Isaiah 64:6 clearly shows us that any kind of righteousness we might earn through our own goodness would be about as valuable as a filthy rag!

Most people live life backwards: they try to earn righteousness through making good choices. But God wants it to be just the opposite. He wants us to make right choices that reflect holiness because of the righteousness of Christ that we identify with. When we are in Him, we are full and therefore able to make wise choices. And when we miss it, we have the supreme benefit of being able to run to Him and ask for forgiveness, knowing that He has already made a way to restore and heal us.

drill it down

As I grew in Christ, I really grasped and understood the concept of being a "new creation." (2 Corinthians 5:17) However, I definitely did not understand that the things of my former life of bondage would be coming back to try to take me over again because I hadn't dealt with them using the full counsel of Scripture. If I was the prostitute in the analogy above, imagine my former pimp cruisin' around the White House trying to convince me to get back into his car. That sounds pretty silly, doesn't it?

Now, as the First Lady, I have authority to tell that loser to leave, and even get him arrested ten different ways. But if there is any lure in my heart that is undealt-with, I may be tempted to go talk to him. I may try to reason with him to get him to see that my new life is so much better. I may spend just a little bit of time with him because there is part of me that is unfamiliar and uncomfortable with the growth my new life demands. And all of those things give him an opportunity to suck me back into the way I used to live. Let me speak frankly to say that as a young woman I had *issues*. Maybe I didn't use drugs, party, or hang out with the wrong crowd, but the issues were present, lurking, and often on the threshold of consuming my sanity. Of course I didn't let anyone know these things, not even my

When something emotional or unexpected surfaces in your life, pursue God for understanding about which primary emotional need lies underneath it.

closest friends or youth leaders. Not that they didn't suspect something was up with my retarded behavior, but most likely they attributed it to the lack of parenting I received and some immaturity. I was great at putting on a big smile and being a ray of sunshine. That was my part, and I had figured out that following the script could make me popular and successful. And it worked—for several years!

I even had myself convinced that my life was great, and despite some hardship as a child, I was going to be a world-changer. There was only one problem. My issues of emotional abandonment and abuse had never been dealt with—never even been talked about other than a brief statement of "testimony" a handful of times.

Somehow, some way, God led me to my Jesse, who became my husband when I was 25 years old. By the prompting of the Holy Spirit, I knew I was to walk out my courtship with him being totally honest about my past. I was so sick of hiding my wounds and pretending they weren't there. That was the beginning of a season of real emotional and spiritual healing in my life, one strengthened by a healthy church where I could be discipled. I walked through Neil Anderson's *Freedom in Christ* program with some amazing women of God who helped me see that the issues I had been trying to ignore and shoo away were only waiting to be confessed, taken authority over, and renounced in the name of Jesus. Only then could I begin to grow in the emotional health God had for me.

Many young woman stuff their emotional scars and wounds down day after day, year after year, thinking that distancing themselves from the pain will make them feel free. But that's not how true freedom is found. I suppressed my pain for over a decade after I came to Christ. All it did was stuff my closet so full that whenever an emotional trigger happened (and they will, that's just life) my closet would explode in unexplained pain, sorrow, or anger.

When I mentor young women, one of the things I say over and over is "drill it down." That means when something emotional or unexpected surfaces in your life, pursue God for understanding about which primary emotional need lies underneath it. For example, I was a good kid in school, but on the rare occasion that a teacher needed to correct me or reprimand me, I would find myself instantly welling up with tears—a response disproportionate to the trigger.

Later in life, when I learned how to drill it down, I realized that my emotional rejection by my parents was quite unresolved and would come out whenever I felt that anyone in authority was anything less than pleased with me. That unresolved emotional need for affirmation and encouragement from my parents surfaced in my life over and over in many different ways, over two decades of my life. When I finally uncovered that truth with one of my own mentors, I was able to fully acknowledge the pain in a prayer that extended forgiveness and grace to my parents. Healing of that issue followed as I continued to seek God and grow in Him.

put into action

If your identity and value is wrapped up in anything other than who you are in Christ, you will find yourself making really bad choices, again and again. Only when you are complete and secure in Christ can you make choices that reflect the fullness of who He is in you. Spend a moment looking back on your life, asking God to show you where you have looked to other sources for your value. List those false sources here:

1. _____

2. _____

3. _____

4. _____

Now that you know these sources are false, how will you change the ways you've become dependent on them? What steps can you take?

_____

_____

_____

_____

_____

_____

Following is a list of "Who I am In Christ" Scriptures. I encourage you to read this list out loud and begin to get these truths down in your heart![14]

I AM ACCEPTED

John 1:12	I am God's child.
John 15:15	I am Christ's friend.
Romans 5:1	I have been justified.
1 Corinthians 6:17	I am united with the Lord (one spirit).
1 Corinthians 6:19-20	I am bought with a price; I belong to God.
1 Corinthians 12:27	I am a member of Christ's Body.
Ephesians 1:1	I am a saint.
Ephesians 2:18	I have access to God through the Holy Spirit.
Colossians 1:14	I have been redeemed and forgiven.
Colossians 2:10	I am complete in Christ.

I AM SECURE

Romans 8:1-2	I am free forever from condemnation.
Romans 8:28	I am assured all things work together for my good.
Romans 8:31-34	I am free from any charge against me.
Romans 8:35-39	I cannot be separated from the love of God.
2 Corinthians 1:21-22	I am established, anointed, and sealed by God.
Colossians 3:3	I am hidden with Christ in God.
Philippians 1:6	I am confident that the good work God has begun in me will be perfected.
Philippians 3:20	I am a citizen of heaven.
2 Timothy 1:7	I have not been given a spirit of fear, but of power, love, and a sound mind.
Hebrews 4:16	I can find grace and mercy in time of need.
1 John 5:18	I am born of God; the evil one cannot touch me.

I AM SIGNIFICANT

Matthew 5:13-14	I am the salt and light of the earth.
John 15:1-5	I am a branch of the true vine, a channel of His life.
John 15:16	I have been chosen and appointed to bear fruit.
Acts 1:8	I am a personal witness of Christ.
1 Corinthians 3:16	I am God's temple.
2 Corinthians 5:17-21	I am a minister of reconciliation for God.
2 Corinthians 6:1	I am God's co-worker
Ephesians 2:6	I am seated with Christ in the heavenly realm.
Ephesians 2:10	I am God's workmanship.
Ephesians 3:12	I may approach God with freedom and confidence.
Philippians 4:13	I can do all things through Christ who strengthens me.

"So teach us to number our days,
that we may gain a heart of wisdom."
Psalm 90:12

chapter 6 smart girls take the long view

one night of poor judgement

Katie was a young woman with a seemingly bright future. At 22 years of age, she was the reigning Miss Nevada, about to compete in the Miss USA pageant. Suddenly, raunchy pictures of her surfaced on the Internet, and Katie's world came to a crashing halt. Photos of her topless and simulating sexual acts with others put her crown and Miss USA eligibility in jeopardy and publicly humiliated her. The story spread quickly—she was all over the news.

Katie hoped to receive mercy from the Miss USA organization (run by billionaire Donald Trump) and made a public apology to that end. She said the photos were taken during an isolated incident from her teenage years. "I am so sorry this happened," she said during a public press conference. "So many of us don't realize how our actions, even one night of poor judgment, can affect the rest of our lives." How true.

She was not given mercy by Miss USA and was indeed stripped of her crown and title as Miss Nevada. When the news broke about Mr. Trump's decision, I watched curiously for Katie's reaction. I wondered how it would all play out and what kind of character she would display. She was not given a second chance, and naturally, she was devastated. And pretty outraged. Honestly, I wasn't surprised at her reaction. Even during her original apology press conference, the lesson she urged young women to learn from her mistake was, "Never let your guard down about being photographed."[15] *Huh?!?* How about, "Don't engage in promiscuous behavior that compromises your value and dignity as a woman." How about, "Live in the light and own the mistakes of your past, or they will find you anyway." Nope. Instead, she basically counseled the young women of America to not get caught on film. Ridiculous.

A few years passed and another young beauty pageant contestant found herself in hot water over a similar situation, but this time the young lady was allowed to keep her crown for whatever reason. Of course the media turned to the former Miss Nevada for a reaction.

I hoped that maybe a few years of life on the other side of fame had helped Katie learn how to present herself more maturely. I was disappointed. Katie indicated how furious she was at the unfair treatment, and then pointed a finger of blame at Donald Trump saying she hoped he knew what he had "put her through" these past few years.[16] *What?* She was the one who got "semi-nude" and crazy, not him. Sadly, she failed to see that she was living with the consequences of her own decisions. Her fate was the result of her own foolishness, and Donald Trump had the authority and the right to pull her crown, whether or not it seemed "fair" to Katie.

Let's go back to something Katie said that reflected wisdom. "So many of us don't realize how our actions, even one night of poor judgment, can affect the rest of our lives." If you really understood where life would

If you really understood where life would take you in God's perfect will, you wouldn't make decisions that could potentially compromise that destiny.

take you in God's perfect will, you wouldn't make decisions that could potentially compromise that destiny.

Instead of risking everything for a momentary thrill of danger, allow yourself to take the long view of your life. You identified some of the purposes that your life potentially holds at the end of the first chapter. What will you sacrifice in order to see those purposes realized?

temporal vs. eternal

Peer pressure exists at every stage of life, but no doubt it is most prevalent (and dangerous) during the adolescent and young adult years. If you like to have the dangerous kind of fun and live recklessly, you won't have to look far for opportunities to do so. What would it cost you to give up those opportunities? You might have fewer "friends." (This word is in quotes because the people who encourage you to do things that are harmful to you don't really care about you.) You might not be popular in school. You might not get into the sorority. Those things may seem really big at a certain phase of your life, but in the grand scheme of your entire lifetime, they are but for a moment.

A young lady complained to me about not having a cell phone like all of her friends. She was from a family that was really struggling financially, and no one else in her family had a cell phone. She was preparing for her first year of college and working a minimum-wage job to save every cent. I talked with her about seeing the long view, being willing to give up things that are temporal to lay hold of her destiny that had eternal implications. Some of her friends who weren't going to college were working the same minimum-wage jobs to pay for their phones, their cars, and their apartments. While all that freedom seemed so appealing to a teenager crossing the threshold into adulthood, I encouraged her to understand that the reality of having all those things now would not offer freedom over the long haul. Getting her education would offer her prolonged freedom from low-paying jobs and being tempted to accumulate "things" she couldn't really afford.

It's tragic to see young people give up a lifetime of destiny for one night or even one moment of poor judgment. Seventeen-year-old Sierra from a tiny town in Missouri traded momentary fun for a lifetime of consequences when she got behind the wheel of a car while intoxicated. She lost control of the vehicle and it overturned, ejecting and killing her 17-year-old passenger and friend, Jessica. Sierra was charged with manslaughter, a crime with a sentence of up to seven years in prison. What an awful fate for a young woman to face. Not only does she have to live with the guilt of her friend's death, something she can never change, but she also has to live with the consequences of her actions and how they will affect her future. All because of one night, a night built on a string of several mistakes, a night where she took her eyes off her long-term purpose for the sake of short-term "fun." This kind of situation and the regret that goes with it can change a woman into someone she was never meant to be. Only the hope and redemption of Christ can bring healing to extreme pain like that.

compartmentalization

What if Sierra had made it home safely that night? Thousands of teenagers miraculously do after similar situations. Would she have realized the danger she put herself and her friend in? Many young people look back on brushes with danger like that and think, "Close call." But few look at that situation, drill it down, and determine what caused them to do something so foolish in the first place. It's like they take the experience, lock it up in a compartment in their mind, and vow to themselves (or God), "I'll never do *that* again." However, the issues that caused the poor judgment in the first place remain and will resurface. Rarely do young people realize that the compartment they locked the irresponsible choice up in has holes in the bottom that leak into every area of their life.

Our culture has created a huge issue by promoting compartmentalization—the notion that your personal character can be divided up into compartments, some of which show responsibility, some of which provide a license for recklessness. We saw it when the former President of the United States, Bill Clinton, was in impeachment proceedings for his private and adulterous escapades with Monica Lewinski. Many people felt his private behavior should hold no bearing on his ability to hold public office. I couldn't get past the fact that if he would lie to his own wife (who could seriously kick his butt and humiliate him publicly), of course he would lie to the anonymous constituents he proposed to represent as president.

Many young women operate their life under the same false notion that each area can be kept separate. One might think, "I am responsible and get good grades, so it's no big deal if I lie to my parents every once in awhile." As a teenager, I would have been the poster-child for this mentality. I assumed my responsible qualities counteracted my foolishness, helping my character to "break even." Does God think that way?

One thing I've noticed about women who compartmentalize their character is that they are smart enough to downplay the foolish compartments. They know deep inside that these areas of stupidity

111

don't please God and appear irresponsible to others, so they keep them hidden to anyone who might have enough maturity to assess the situation accurately. They'll party and live foolish in front of their peers, but in front of their youth pastor they paint themselves as mature girls who are headed in the right direction. But God doesn't celebrate that kind of half-hearted devotion. Jesus' words are clear to us in Matthew 22:37-40 as He reminded a group of religious people that whole-hearted devotion was the Lord's first commandment, "You shall love the LORD your God with *all* your heart, with *all* your soul, and with *all* your mind."

Your life is all one canvas, and if you're a Christian, it all belongs to the Lord. He's not okay with "hidden" areas of rebellion (and nothing is hidden from Him anyway, so you may as well give it up!). There shouldn't be a "going to school" you, a "church" you, and an "alone with my friends" you. You should just be "you" in every area of your life. It's called integrity. It means you show the same character in every situation. He wants *all* of your heart.

Even in the case of Miss Nevada, I question the logic and excuse of the "isolated incident." It's possible. But after mentoring young women for over fifteen years, a more likely explanation is that a root issue is underneath the behavior that led to Katie's mistake. I'll be honest, I've seen the pictures of Katie that she says "ruined her life," and they depict a young woman who seemed comfortable and confident—smile after smile, picture after picture. They sort of made me scratch my head and wonder what was isolated about that night—that it was caught on film? Was that the only night in her life she had consumed one too many alcoholic beverages? Was that the only night in her life she was foolish enough to brazenly act out sexual situations (with both boys and girls)?

To be a woman of wisdom, you should make integrity your aim. There is no such thing as an isolated incident. Every moment and action

is tied to who you know yourself to be in
Christ and what you believe. Poor character
will come and find you in the end no matter how
hard you try to hide it. Don't let moments filled
with temporal pleasures be traded for a lifetime of
consequences that could affect your ability to walk in
God's destiny for your life.

Every moment and action is tied to who you know yourself to be in Christ and what you believe.

living in the light

You are not expected to be perfect. Only God is perfect. When
my husband and I were in pastoral ministry, we would tell our team, "We
do not expect you to be perfect, but we do expect you to live in the light."
That meant we had to live it as well. When we blew it, it was not time to run
and hide. It was time to confess and forsake our sin, no matter how severe
the consequences.

Not only do I really value honesty, but I see that God commands
living in the light in order to have authentic relationships with others and
with Him. 1 John 1:7 says, "If we walk in the light as He is in the light, we
have fellowship with one another and the blood of Jesus Christ His Son
cleanses us from all sin."

There will be times in your life where you miss it. You may even
miss it big time like Miss Nevada, and your sin may threaten the destiny
God has called you to. But if you fear the Lord, as we talked about in the
last chapter, you'll care more about being right with God then protecting
your reputation or the consequences that may come from honesty. This is
not an easy pill to swallow. Trust me, I have had to live in the light despite
tremendous pain. I have had to stand under the weight of hundreds of

people knowing about weaknesses in my personal life. It is not easy. But when you bring sin or shame into the light, it dies. Living in the light is the only way to guarantee that missteps do not take you hostage.

When you bring failures and sin into the light, you are actually strengthening your future in the Lord, although our fleshly understanding feels like it's just the opposite. The lie is that if nobody knows, I can preserve or control my future... nothing has to change. The *reality* is that if you hide your weaknesses, sin, and personal shame from others, they will grow and begin to take over your future, bossing you into faulty coping mechanisms to keep up the façade. Then you will be at the mercy of the sin you are trying to cover, which leads to everything spinning out of control.

Luke 8:17 says, "For all that is secret will eventually be brought into the open, and everything that is concealed will be brought to light and made known to all." (NLT) If you try to hide, your sin will find you out. Confess your sin by bringing it into the light, and God will cover you. He will replace shame with a new sense of peace knowing you have been put right. Just like Sophie from the previous chapter, who found new life after her DUI, God offers hope to all who will stand in the grace He gives for the forgiveness of sin.

start at the very beginning

In the classic movie "The Sound of Music," Julie Andrews sings, "Start at the very beginning, a very good place to start." If you want to make wise choices, you too need to start at the very beginning. It is much easier to

114

make good choices when you go into situations with your head on straight from the beginning. Stupidity has a way of snowballing, so be very mindful of how you start something.

A wise woman and highly acclaimed sexual abstinence speaker named Pam Stenzel told a story commonly played out in every high school across America. A 16-year-old girl approached Pam after a school assembly to admit that she'd slept with a guy, and she wasn't sure where he'd been. Pam tells her, "You've got to get tested. Don't wait, do it right away." The girl took her advice, got tested, and found out she had HPV (which can cause cervical cancer, remember?). She called Pam in tears to tell her the story.

A few months back, she had been invited to a party. She and some friends decided to go. While they were there, they had a few drinks. She got drunk, and she had sex with a guy she didn't really know. Not much to the story, really. Now she's living with a lifetime of consequences.

This story repeats itself over and over every weekend among high school and college populations. And it clearly illustrates the importance of decisions, especially small ones. That 16-year-old girl made three crucial decisions that fateful night: 1) to go to a party, 2) to drink, 3) to have sex. Usually the first decision in a sequence like this one is the easiest to make, and the most critical. This girl's tragic mistake wasn't just in the decision to have sex. It was in her decision to drink, too, because no doubt intoxication aided in the lapse of judgment. But her folly was first in her decision to go to a party where crazy stuff like that happens. If she had just stayed home, she would have avoided the pressure to drink and have sex. Choosing not to go to the party would have been the easiest decision of the three, too. Unfortunately, she didn't choose wisely.

It's very common for one stupid decision to lead to another, which leads to another. Before you know it, foolishness has snowballed all around you, and then you feel trapped with no way out. It's so important to make smart decisions on the small stuff, because it will keep you from heading in the wrong direction.

Pam Stenzel often tells girls who are completely overwhelmed at the news of an unplanned pregnancy that all their choices from here on out will be hard ones. She tries to show them the reality of the choices they face— keeping the child and forfeiting your teenage years to be a parent, giving the child to someone else to raise, and, unfortunately, the very prevalent choice of abortion (which causes certain emotional scarring). These all carry life-long consequences. Pam reminds them, "You had an easy choice. It was way back there when you were deciding whether you were going to have sex." [17]

I often think about what led me to live outside of God's will in a disobedient romantic relationship with my prom date for so many years after high school. If I go back to the very beginning, I can see that my choice to go to the senior prom with someone I barely knew was the easiest choice for me to make, and that's where I had the best chance to do the right thing. Honestly, pride had gotten in my way because I didn't want to go to prom alone. I wanted someone to ask me, but no one did. So I took matters into my own hands, along with some help from an innocent friend, and I got set up. What if I had prayed about that choice? I could have saved my prom date and myself a few years of heartache.

the false notion of fate

Some people think that "fate" is ultimately responsible for our destiny in life. Even some Christians believe that, only they call fate "God." It's amazing how many people subscribe to this belief even unknowingly. It's commonly seen in the ideal that each person has one person they're destined to marry on this planet, and "fate" will bring them together. So, if it doesn't happen it "wasn't meant to be." It makes for a good movie plot, but it doesn't make for good theology. A lot of things that God wants to happen on this earth don't ever happen because He depends upon the will of people to carry those things out. Another way "fate" is commonly blamed is when something goes wrong in a person's life. Instead of looking at what that person may have done to get themselves in the mess, they'll act like there was nothing they could do to avoid it.

Clearly, God is not a "fate-ist." From the very beginning of the world, He proved how important choice and free will decision-making were to Him. He gave Adam and Eve a simple choice to make in the Garden of Eden, and then He gave them instruction on which choice to make—"Do not eat from the Tree of the Knowledge of Good and Evil." He didn't force them not to eat from that tree. He didn't put an invisible deflector shield around it to prevent the sin from devastating humanity. Surely He knew the grave consequences that would be a result of their disobedience. Yet, He still allowed them to choose. Most of us would agree, the fall of humankind was because of free will, not fate.

It's important that we clear up the fate issue to fully understand God's role as it pertains to decision-making. God created you to make decisions, not to blow off your responsibility and blame it on fate, or even worse—on Him! We even turn our insecurities into issues of fate. "I'm just not meant to be a good student. It's too hard for me. Maybe I should drop out." Too often learning disabilities, difficult family dynamics, at-risk environments, and even poor stewardship are

A lot of things that God wants to happen on this earth don't ever happen because He depends upon the will of those people to carry those things out.

117

to blame for situations like these. Instead of admitting our weaknesses and seeking the Lord or leaders for help, we grow insecure and blame it on some cosmic force we cannot control.

Here's a statement you can find proof for all throughout God's Word: It is God's will for you to succeed. That isn't to say that difficulty and suffering aren't part of the Christian life. So what do I mean by "succeed"? I mean, overcome, grow, rise above, and live in the peace that God provides (even when life sucks!). This may not be your experience, and I can relate, because I lived there for a couple of decades. But that doesn't mean it's God's fault. And because He loves you so much, He wants to help you succeed. Ask Him what piece of the puzzle you're missing. Ask Him to show you why you're not overcoming and growing in certain areas. Everyone deals with failure and pain; they are facts of life. But if these things are the recurring themes of your life, it's time to stop blaming God and ask Him for mercy and grace to help you start digging out. There is hope for you. It's never too late.

put into action

Taking the long view means you will have to live today as if it really matters. What heartaches in your life can you link to small choices back at the beginning? List examples of sin you see in your life that can be traced back to a single choice.

1. _____

2. _____

3. _____

Finally, are you willing to live in the light about these items as well as other sin that is present in your life? Write down the name of two or three trusted friends or leaders who you could confess your sin to. Try to think of people who are strong enough spiritually to help you overcome reoccurring sin in the future.

1. _____

2. _____

3. _____

"Keep your heart with all diligence,
for out of it spring the issues of life."
Proverbs 4:23

chapter 7 smart girls guard their hearts

nothing more than feelings

Julie, a new bride, called me in a panic. "He says he doesn't love me anymore. How can that be true?" We talked for a long time about the hurtful things that had been flying out of her and her new husband's mouth. Unfortunately, the short timeline of their courtship and engagement meant the significant emotional challenges of marriage had been dealt with only superficially in pre-marital counseling. Now they were faced with how to work through the surfacing negative feelings in light of the vows they had taken just six months previous. Sadly, their marriage ended very painfully just before what would have been their one-year anniversary, even though they had a new baby on the way. No relationship can last when it is based on mere feelings. Feelings come and go.

Philippians 1:9-10 says, "Learn to love appropriately. You need to use your head and test your feelings so that your love is sincere and intelligent, not sentimental gush." (MSG) A few years ago while reading this verse, the Holy Spirit spoke something that riveted me. He said, "Your feelings are *unreliable*." I then started to evaluate how many of my decisions as a young person were made based on feelings. No wonder I made so many stupid choices!

Now, feelings aren't a bad thing—God created them, after all. But we have to remember that our feelings don't always reflect reality. They reflect things from our perspective, which is not always necessarily God's perspective.

When I counseled a teenage couple that they shouldn't be saying "I love you" a few months into their relationship, they were confused. "But I do love her," said the 18-year-old boy. The truth is, he had feelings that he interpreted as love, but they were not based on God's definition of love. God's love is a giving love. It's sacrificial. It goes to great lengths to serve others and deny self. The reality of this relationship (which eventually came out) is that both the young man and the young woman were gratifying their own selfish needs for acceptance, security, and even physical pleasure. They had misinterpreted emotional and physical attraction as love. The relationship drew them both out of God's will for a long and painful season. They caused each other to stumble morally, and they damaged each other's destiny. Does that sound like God's giving kind of love?

Feelings reflect things from our perspective, which is not always necessarily God's perspective.

That doesn't mean that all your feelings are bad. They aren't. In fact, one of the most important life lessons I learned as an adult is that feelings by themselves are neither good nor bad—they just are.[18] And they are not always reliable. Sometimes they happen to line up with God's perfect will for us, which is great. My love for my husband is an example of that. The feelings I have for him line up with what God has planned for me—a solid marriage. However, there have been times in my life where my feelings have directly contradicted what God wanted for me. There were times where I was so deeply hurt by my husband that I couldn't muster up one feeling of love for him. But that didn't mean I was running for a divorce lawyer. I knew that the feelings of hurt I was experiencing would pass as God worked forgiveness and redemption into our marriage, and He did! Good thing I didn't act on my unreliable feelings; my life as well as my husband's and my children's lives would have been forever altered, and unnecessarily so.

Sometimes feelings are accurate, and sometimes they're not. You just can't rely on them; that's all there is to it.

Sometimes feelings are accurate, and sometimes they're not. You just can't rely on them; that's all there is to it.

Since feelings are so unreliable, it stands to reason they should be included in the "everything" that Scripture encourages us to test. "Test everything. Hold onto the good." (1 Thessalonians. 5:21) Think about what you've learned in science about the scientific method. Scientific facts start out as theories. Then they are tested, and through the tests, the theory is proven either reliable or unreliable. It's the same with your feelings. Feelings are nothing more than a theory; they are not facts. In order to discover what's true and reliable, we need to test them.

How do we test them? By the counsel of the Word of God, first and foremost. Does this feeling line up with what God says? Secondly, we test feelings by the objective wisdom from others more mature in their faith. Sometimes I don't even know what it is that I'm feeling, and getting wise counsel from others who can point me to the Word is really helpful.

When a 16-year-old girl tells me school is lame, and she wants to drop out, I can't help but point out that this decision would be based on feelings. Her feelings are deceiving her into thinking life will be *easier* if she just quits—but the exact opposite is true. No matter how lame she thinks school is, life will be *much* harder if she chooses not to complete high school. If she tests her feelings against Scripture, it would be clear that dropping out does not reflect wisdom. Throughout the Bible, God instructs us to do things that are difficult, to endure in the darkest seasons, and to do whatever we're called to with all of our heart, trusting in the Lord. If she asked other mature believers about dropping out, they could help point her to that truth. They could help her uncover the root problems that are making her want to quit. As we learned before, those root issues will just come out somewhere else if they aren't taken care of.

In Neil Anderson's book, *Victory Over the Darkness* he states, "What kind of life would you live if you believed what you felt instead of the truth? Your life would be as inconsistent as your feelings."[19] Amen, Neil. You just described the entire high school experience for most teenagers.

An inconsistent life is not what God wants for you. Being governed by the truth of God's Word is the only way to overcome the pull to be led about by our up-and-down feelings.

Being governed by the truth of God's Word is the only way to overcome the pull to be led about by our up-and-down feelings.

your heart matters

As humans, and especially as women, we instinctively understand our feelings to be products of our hearts. But most of us don't process our feelings in the light of the boundaries of God's Word. In fact, I would venture to say that the vast majority of people swear a subconscious oath of loyalty to "follow their hearts" wherever they may lead them. This kind of aimless wandering gets us in trouble. Our hearts need boundaries in order to stay protected and full of wisdom.

Did you know that your heart (your mind, will, and emotions) is one of the most valuable treasures you possess? And if you think for one minute the enemy (the devil) is going to leave your treasure alone, think again. The Bible tells you to guard your heart above everything else in Proverbs 4:23 because it is the "wellspring of life." That means it's the source of your life—it determines how healthy or polluted your life will be. Your heart matters!

A young lady confessed a sexual incident to me, one that cost her the virginity she had fought for nineteen years to protect. She knew it was a horrible mistake and seemed repentant. Being swayed by affection from boys was definitely an ongoing temptation for her (a "root" issue stemming from a life of abuse and rejection as a child). We had talked previously about the measures she would have to take to keep her heart guarded from the manipulation of boys, but she was struggling with seeing the true intentions of ones who paid her unsolicited and inappropriate attention. Her heart was a revolving door letting anyone in. In order for her to actually walk in victory in this area of temptation, she was going to have to get downright mad. Mad at the devil for all of the countless ways he had ripped her off. Mad at boys who wouldn't leave her alone and respect the boundaries she was trying to put in place (however feeble those attempts may have been).

I asked this young lady, "How would you respond if it were your 15-year-old sister confessing this incident to you?" Without hesitation, she said, "I would find the guy and cut off his hands." Her answer revealed the intense love and protection she had for her little sister. She cared more about her sister's heart being invaded than she did about her own. "How can you not feel that same way about your own heart?" I asked her. Silence and tears followed.

the garden

I heard an analogy once that proved extremely helpful in understanding the way we guard our hearts. Imagine your heart to be a garden that you've lovingly planted. It might include fruits and vegetables to provide you nourishment in the days ahead, or it might grow beautiful flowers—the kind that need to be carefully nurtured and meticulously tended to.

A garden like that should have fencing around it to keep out uncaring passersby. You don't want the neighborhood kids tromping through your garden because it's a shortcut to the park. You don't want dogs digging bones in your garden or eating your produce. Yes, you'll need something to keep this kind of traffic out. A six-foot privacy fence would be a little extreme, since you'd like to share the beauty of your garden with your friends and neighbors. The kind of fence you're looking for is one that allows people to look in to your garden, but also one that allows them in by invitation only, through a gate that you alone lock and unlock.

Your heart is much the same. Some women, after being wounded, build cement walls around their hearts, allowing no one in. Others just get used to pieces and parts being picked off by intruders and no longer steward what God wants to grow in the garden of their heart. Our hearts should be carefully nurtured and tended to, while also being protected against predators and invaders. Safe people will ask before they come in. A friend will even sit and pull weeds with you while you share conversation. The people who you let in should only want your garden to become more delightful.

Guarding your heart is not just about romance. It's not just about boys or relationships either. Guarding your heart means that you apply the boundaries of God's Word to your feelings and emotions so that your garden can be tended to deliberately, that it may become fruitful and beautiful. You will need to guard your heart from all kinds of things throughout the course of your lifetime. Bitterness, jealousy, depression, offense—these are things that should not be allowed to grow in your garden, and regular weeding will keep them out. But you must also be on the watch for shady perpetrators who are out to destroy and violate your heart. Beware! The enemy will invite all kinds of abusers into your life if you leave your gate unlocked.

take it all the way

Although guarding your heart has to do with all aspects of your feelings measured against God's truth, boys and romantic relationships seem to dominate the landscape on the roads you are learning to navigate. Since this topic has derailed more women than I can stand to count, we will spend the rest of our chapter addressing this important subject. (YES! A whole chapter about sex and boys!)

God has already given you the roadmap to success in relationships by laying out clear guidelines in Scripture. The Bible clearly teaches to honor others, abstain from fleshly lusts, and avoid sexual encounters outside of a marriage covenant. However, if your judgment is so clouded that these principles are of no consequence to you, simply evaluate the potential outcomes of your choices to see where dating relationships and sex will lead you.

According to the Center for Disease Control (CDC), forty-six percent of highschoolers have already had sex, and roughly half of those are currently infected with an STD. It used to be the case that only those who had multiple sexual experiences were likely to contract an STD, but times have changed. A young woman can be infected with a serious disease during her very first sexual encounter, and it doesn't even need to be intercourse. Most teenage girls are deathly afraid of getting pregnant, so they will do just about anything sexually other than intercourse to avoid this fate. Many young women either disregard or are completely unaware of the fact that skin-on-skin contact can still transmit the serious virus called HPV, a virus that can cause cervical cancer in women. Not only that, but I've met a handful of women in my life who have gotten pregnant without having intercourse (I know you don't believe me, but it's true).

A young woman can be infected with a serious disease during her very first sexual encounter, and it doesn't even need to be intercourse.

The truth of the Bible should be your moral compass if you are a Christian. However, if you are not, I encourage you to imagine the consequences of your choices as they may play out, and take that scenario all the way to the end. For example, if you are considering having sex with someone, think about all that may come out of that choice. You may get pregnant (even if you use a condom—happened to me at the conception of my second son). If you were to get pregnant, would you... get an abortion, keep the baby and most likely become a single parent, or give the baby up for adoption? What would God want you to do? After the choice to have sex has been made, and conception is confirmed, all of the resulting choices are extremely difficult and carry with them life-long consequences.

Let's say you dodge the bullet of unwanted pregnancy. The odds are still stacked against you, because if you have sex you are likely to get an STD. Sexually transmitted diseases are not just "inconvenient," they carry serious consequences such as cancer and infertility. The CDC states clearly on their web site, "The surest way to avoid transmission of STDs is to abstain from sexual intercourse."[20] The deception of the enemy and the American teenage culture paints abstinence as antiquated and uncool. On the contrary, the *truth* is it's the only smart choice a young woman can make to preserve her own healthy future.

Part of that future may likely include the beautiful mystery of sex within God's boundaries—marriage. This covenantal act has the power of redemption, worship, and true ecstasy, spirit, soul and body, because it is free from shame. No matter what your sexual past may be like, this can be part of your future. But not if you do whatever you feel like doing in the here and now.

dating? harmless?

"But I don't want to have *sex*," you might say. "I just want a boyfriend. What's the harm in that?"

I've had the benefit of watching hundreds of young lives play out over the course of fifteen or more years, as well as hearing the stories of those who have been in ministry twice that long. I've seen lots of approaches to the subject of dating by pastoral leaders, and I've had the opportunity to observe the outcomes over the years. My husband and I have felt with prophetic urgency the need to teach this generation about *not* dating (gasp!), especially not the world's way. Unfortunately, that viewpoint was not always met with a lot of support, and we were even asked not to share our views at times by some parents and leaders who felt it was too controversial. It seems the adults think it's a sticky subject.

Over the years we've seen many girls go off the deep end as the result of dating relationships. Several got pregnant. Some of them parented, often alone. Some of them had abortions. These situations are by no means unredeemable, but they definitely make the top of the list of things more difficult than you can imagine. And many of these stressed-out young women have been derailed from their destiny by not responding to the Lord's redemptive call. They are still floundering.

Is dating harmless? I guess that depends on what kind of dating you're talking about. A 25-year-old who wants to see clearly the character and spiritual strength of a potential marriage partner could harmlessly go to coffee, ask lots of questions, and spend time in group settings getting to know that person. A 15-year-old who spends hours of unaccounted for time at her boyfriend's house while his parents are not home... now that's a different story. Very few teenage relationships can survive without the cornerstone of physical intimacy, and there's a reason why. Fifteen-year-olds who are attracted to one another generally don't have the emotional and relational capacity to fill up the vast amounts of time they typically spend with each other. "Just talking" or "just hanging out" gives way to making out, which gives way to foreplay. And foreplay is a really hard train to stop once the fire has been lit. Sex *will* follow unless the relationship is severed. It's only a matter of time. That is precisely why the Bible clearly warns, "not to awaken love before the time is right." (Song of Solomon 2:7, NLT)

purity or privacy

Some young women have the distinct benefit of parents who will teach them how to guard their heart from inappropriate romance at an early age. These parents will set boundaries and mandate that they are upheld, or consequences will follow. However, the growing trend in most American homes (even Christian ones) is a lassez-faire, or "hands-off," approach. Many parents give their teenage children too much privacy and too much independence at too young of an age. They also place undue responsibility on their teenagers when they themselves are unwilling to uphold their own parental responsibility to train their children to be successful in relationships. It's easier and more convenient to "let them figure it out."

I've seen the following scenario play out many times: A teenage girl is allowed to date a young man who the parents do not know that well. She is trusted to spend time with him alone, be in romantic settings, and function completely as a "couple" in many aspects. However, when things go too far (and they often do) the girl either confesses or is found out, and her parents are devastated, furious, and confused at how this happened.

Privacy is not a teenager's primary need. Where is "privacy" talked about in the Bible? One woman I know, after being caught in her jeans and a bra in her room with her boyfriend as a teenager, consequently was grounded and lost her bedroom door for an entire year. Even though she was furious at the time, she now appreciates the tenacity of her parents to protect her from her own stupidity. And on her wedding day, she wore that white gown with pride, a 27-year-old virgin, knowing her parents had saved her from major regret, heartache, and who knows what else. What's more important to you, purity or privacy?

What's more important to you, purity or privacy?

the diamond in you

Several years ago, I heard a life-changing message from a woman named Dr. Wanda Turner. She had been in pastoral ministry for decades, survived the infidelity and premature death of a husband, and believed in the faithfulness of God no matter what season she found herself in. I was smart enough to get the recording of a message she preached at a women's conference, sensing that I would need its timeless truths. Since then, that recording has been duplicated many times over, by myself and others, and found its way into women's hands of all walks of life all over the globe. We refer to it as "the diamond message."

Here's the gist of it. You are valuable. You are God's precious jewel, worth far more than any diamond or precious stone. Miss Wanda, in her delightful banter, describes the diamonds in the display windows at jewelry stores as "a bunch of junk" because of all the lights, glass and mirrors it takes to make them brilliant enough to attract you. The really good stuff, the most expensive in the store, is kept in the back, locked in a safe on some dark velvet. That's *you*.

Does the diamond get to set its worth? No, the owner does—he decides. And if a half-working man (or teenage *boy*) tries to come in and buy a valuable diamond, the owner is going to ask him, "How much are you willing to pay?" The right answer is not, "Well, can I get a discount for going to church twice a year? I mean, I'm working on getting some money together and everything, but I just don't know yet." The owner will reply, "She's not the one for you," and put you back in the safe because you're *precious*.

One of my favorite quotes from the diamond message: "Don't go on sale for a man who can't afford you." God sets your price, not you. He's the one who gives consent for you to come out of the safe. And if you really do leave it up to Him, He'll make sure you come out only for a man who is willing to pay full price for you!

When you understand your value to God, your choices in life will reflect that value. Girls who know what they are worth are far less likely to throw their hearts away for a ridiculous high school romance. Smart girls realize the price God paid to ransom them from sin and spiritual darkness. They are guided by a sense of God's purpose for them, and they know that there is no room for wasted days as they move toward that purpose.

a colossal waste of time

When I was a young person I never even considered the fact that God would be interested in my dating life. I figured as long as I followed the "rules" (do not be unequally yoked, and don't have sex before marriage) I could pretty much do what I wanted. I didn't have parents who would shape my point of view on dating after the Lord's perspective. I never even thought to ask my mom what she thought of the whole thing, and she never offered an opinion on the subject either. I figured my dating life was my business. I wasn't living by the truth of the Word—the truth that my life was not my own.

All that being said, I wasted some pretty serious chunks of time as a young person in dating relationships. Some of them were on the "harmless" side, at least as far as the physical relationship goes. But looking back I see that there were many emotionally unhealthy aspects of those relationships, including clinginess and a sense of ownership or entitlement, which caused great harm in the long run. I developed some really ugly expectations through those experiments of immaturity. Even sound teaching at youth group wasn't enough, because I didn't have anyone specifically guiding me—other than my peers who were winging it themselves, that is.

Listen, the chances that you will meet the man you're destined to be with while you're still a teenager (or even in your young twenties) are actually really slim. Even if you happen to know that guy during these years of your youth, it's highly unlikely that God would trust you with that kind of life-changing information at a young age. You just don't need to know right now. And if you're just wanting to "have fun" without worrying about the seriousness of destiny, consider the truth that you can have plenty of fun in co-ed relationships without the complexities and potential temptations of the romantic junk. Don't spend these critical years of destiny pursuit pining away for a boyfriend or going from relationship to relationship. It's a colossal waste of your time.

a marriageable age and stage

I'm not saying that all relationships are of the devil and you should become a nun. A few of you might actually find yourself currently on the threshold of a serious relationship that could be God's will. If you think you may have found "the one," then this section is for you.

I've learned some really important factors for a young woman to consider in determining whether or not she is ready for a romantic relationship unto marriage. This list is not comprehensive, but here are a few things I think are critical. Let me describe a woman who is ready for a season of courtship and marriage:

1. She is of a marriageable age and stage. Meaning, she's not just "technically" a legal adult, over the age of 18. We're talking about someone who actually functions as an adult. She is:

    a. Financially independent of her parents, or at the very least diligently working toward that goal prior to marriage.

    b. Fully employed, managing her own legal responsibilities,

time commitments and bills, as well as able to live on her own. Some women choose to live with their parents in the season prior to marriage in order to wisely steward resources and provide accountability. I think the goal is *readiness*. There should be concern if you have no clue how to live on your own, yet you think you're ready for marriage.

c. On a course to walk out her destiny, whether that includes education, ministry training, or something similar. In other words, she is not just hanging out—she is headed toward a direction from the Lord for her future. (I've seen lots of girls get swayed into heading toward a boy's future, instead of toward her own; and when the relationship ends, as most do, she has to start back at square one.)

2. She not only shows maturity in her decisions, but that maturity is affirmed by the leaders who have a place in her life, including—but not limited to—her parents. Her spiritual maturity is evident in her daily relationship with God and her service to the church.

3. She is ready to walk out a relationship completely in the light, with the input of leaders and peers. Here's a litmus test for you: if you feel uncomfortable talking about physical and emotional boundaries with an interested party, you're not ready to be held accountable to those boundaries. And it's really hard to do it right without accountability.

Now, just because you have all those things above doesn't mean a particular relationship is heaven-sent either. One of my friends married a great guy named Matt. My husband and I referred to him as our church's most eligible bachelor. Before they started their courtship I had three different women (all of them Godly) on three different occasions confide in me that they felt like God was showing them Matt was their husband. I tried to give some advice to the first two about just waiting on the Lord and not pursuing anything in their own strength—that God would bring it up in his heart if it was part of the plan. But by the time bachelorette number three came along, I got really blunt. I told her, "Wow, you're the third girl in a year's time who's told me that." She got the message. God is obviously not going around telling different women that Matt is "the one." Turns out, none of them were right, and Matt married somebody else completely!

no regrets

A guarded heart does not just keep out creeps. A guarded heart will keep out anything that is not God's will for you, even a really great man of God. Some people automatically interpret any kind of favorable circumstances as God's will, instead of asking God himself. But God wants you to pray about every opportunity and crossroad in your life. So even when everything looks "right," a woman with a guarded heart will still bring it to the Lord, especially in relationships.

For example, when I was in my twenties and still single, I met a young man named Chris on a vacation to California. To my astonishment, he was a very strong Christian with a steady job as a high school teacher, solid goals for his life, financial integrity, and a wonderful family. (That's a pretty rare combination, I've found). On top of all that, he had a wonderful personality and was a gentleman in every way. We became friends and "pen pals," sort of (back before email—you know, when dinosaurs roamed the earth). After a second trip to California

A guarded heart will keep out anything that is not God's will for you, even a really great man of God.

to visit him, accompanied by my brother, I had the opportunity to pray about whether or not I was to pursue a relationship with Chris beyond friendship. I just didn't have peace about it, and he respected my hesitation, so we remained friends.

About a year later, my brother felt God leading him to California to pursue a career in the toy industry, and wouldn't you know it, the only person he really knew there was my friend, Chris. In fact, my brother moved in with Chris's family for a time and then became his roommate in their own place. They grew to be very close friends.

I went on to marry my Jesse, and Chris went on to marry a wonderful woman named Jessica. Looking back, I am so glad that I didn't interpret the circumstances under which we met and became friends as some kind of "divine opportunity" for romance to ensue. I now realize that God didn't bring Chris into my life for me. I was merely a bridge. God used my relationship with Chris to bring my brother one of the most loyal and abiding friendships he's had in his life.

And because Chris and I never crossed lines we shouldn't have, our hearts remain completely clean with one another, with no regrets. We can hang out together with our spouses and share stories and laughter with a clean conscience. That is God's idea of Christian community! That's a living example of why the Bible talks about not defrauding your brother or sister (1 Thessalonians 4:3-8).

put into action

Proverbs 14:16 in the New Living Translation says: "The wise are cautious and avoid danger, fools plunge ahead with great confidence." This just isn't a great idea, it's *truth*. If you want to grow into a woman with a guarded heart, be cautious in your relationships, and avoid dangerous situations of romance before the Lord releases you to it. If you want to be foolish, by all means head into every relationship that presents itself at the reckless pace of all your peers. It's your choice.

Think about the situations you've observed or experienced concerning romance at a young age. Answer the questions below to help you make sense of your observations and experiences in light of the truth of what you just read.

1. What is the final state of the longest relationships you've seen or experienced personally? Are the two people still together? If so, what do you think keeps them together? If not, what led to the downfall of the relationship?

   _____

   _____

   _____

   _____

   _____

2. Everyone needs boundaries in order to keep themselves safe from temptation in relationships. What boundaries will help you guard your heart? Ask the Lord what His boundaries are for you, and write them here.

_____

_____

_____

_____

_____

3. How guarded is your heart in relationship situations? Do you recognize any unhealthy patterns that draw you to relationships to satisfy your own emotional needs? If so, what are those patterns? Ask God to help you process your emotions in a healthy way that will keep your heart safe.

_____

_____

_____

_____

_____

_____

_____

_____

_____

_____

"Fools think their own way is right,
but the wise listen to others."
Proverbs 12:15 (NLT)

chapter 8 smart girls take cover

girls just wanna have fun

Jill was a Christian, but a strong-willed teenager. She was hilarious and fun, but also very mischievous and a little on the wild side. She didn't party or anything, but she was known to try almost anything, as long as it got her some laughs and some attention. She tried not to cross biblical lines of morality but pushed those boundaries to the limit often. After wasting a good bit of her high school education not caring about school, she was suddenly confronted with the reality that college was next. She was very bright, but her lack of effort overshadowed her intelligence. Her grades and test scores couldn't get her into the schools she wanted to go to, the ones her friends would be attending, where she knew she could have a lot of fun.

Jill was very lucky to have been raised by Godly and wise parents who saw this as an opportunity to apprehend their daughter's attention and help her lay hold of her destiny. Her parents had both attended a smaller Christian college, and they knew that while their daughter's grades and test scores might not meet the academic standards of the school, they would be close enough to put her on the fence. They also knew that the school admissions office would place great weight on their parental recommendation of the student's potential since they were both alumni and shared the same values as the school. It looked like it would be possible for their daughter to be accepted.

When Jill's parents brought up the option of her attending this small Christian college, she was opposed to it immediately. It was far away and in a small town. She wouldn't know anyone. It didn't sound like her kind of fun at all. Her parents firmly reminded her that her own choices had brought her to this place in her life, and they strongly sensed that God was asking her to lay down her preferences and pray about applying to this school. What other options did she have? Miss life-of-the-party most certainly did not want to stay at home and attend community college or a vocational school. That sounded even less fun.

Thankfully, Jill really respected her parents. Although she didn't always make great choices, she wasn't out to rebel just for the sake of rebellion. She just always wanted to have as much fun as possible! Her parents' words pierced her heart, and she knew she was out of options because of the way she had haphazardly approached school in the past. She knew she could do better, and the crossroads she was at sobered her enough to really pray about her parents' suggestion.

After a few weeks of praying and researching the small college, Jill had a renewed sense of peace growing in her. She felt hope rise in her heart that God would redeem her stupidity concerning school in the past, and she had a firm understanding that her future could be different if she really laid down her own desires for fun to obey God wherever He led her. She asked her parents lots of questions about what they saw for her future, and she did a lot of listening.

She eventually applied to the school, was accepted, and agreed to her parents' condition that they would pay her tuition fully as long as she kept a B average. Any class she got a C or less in she would have to pay them back for.

Jill held up her end of the bargain, graduating in four years with honors, and even went on to pursue a graduate degree in psychology. When asked what prompted her to shift her college plans to attend this school, she replied, "I wanted to honor my parents and what God was saying through them."

How blessed was Jill to have parents to step in and cover her, despite the irresponsible behavior she had shown? How would it have been different if her parents had had the attitude of, "Good luck, honey, I have no clue what to tell you." Jill's parents recognized the potential in her, and they wisely seized the moment of their daughter's predicament of being rejected by her first college choices. They had insight for their daughter about what she needed. They saw options she didn't see or even desire. God used her parents to put Jill on a path to her destiny that she would have completely missed if it were merely up to her. Jill's parents rightly walked in their God-given role as her covering.

God has you covered

When you think of the word "authority," what comes to mind? Like most young people, you probably have images in your mind of police officers, parents, and your school principal. You may not realize that God is the one who created authority and placed people in authority over you for your *benefit*, not to make your life miserable. The people in your life who are responsible for helping to train you spiritually have spiritual authority over you. But what does that mean?

Spiritual authority exists to release potential in others. It's not meant to be a dominating rule-keeping force, but a source of instruction,

Spiritual authority exists to release potential in others.

143

correction, and discipline (when needed) unto spiritual growth. If your parents are Christians, they walk in spiritual authority to help train you to godliness. Other people who have spiritual authority over you are pastors and leaders who you can look to for wisdom and training in life. All of these people are part of the covering God set up to protect you and keep you safe from your own stupid choices.

boundaries

Jesse and I started our dating relationship when we were around 24 years old, and we were separated by about 2,000 miles of distance. Obviously, it was quite easy to keep our physical relationship pure during this time. When I started making plans to move up to Washington to be with him and transition to engagement, we knew we were going to need some extra intervention to help us stay pure. First, we made a list of about 30 rules that we knew we needed to abide by. They included things like curfew, modest dress, no R-rated movies, and locations that were "forbidden" to be alone in—like his apartment. These things were self-imposed boundaries that were necessary to help us in our areas of weakness (which were conveniently and painfully exposed by the mistakes made in previous relationships).

The list Jesse and I made would have been way less effective if we were the only two who knew about it. We were open and honest with our friends about the things on our list, and we knew they would call us on any loopholes we tried to create or any areas of rebellion. In fact, for many months, I connected regularly with a more mature woman of God whom I greatly respect and went through the items on my list with her. It was painful at times, but it sure made me not want to have to go through it again by repeating my mistakes!

What happens when God gives you boundaries and you overstep them? Look at the story in chapter seven of Joshua. Israel had just come off a major victory at the city of Jericho. They had obeyed God, and He miraculously brought the great stone walls around an entire city crashing to the ground. After that victory, He gave specific instructions about how they were to approach the material possessions they had just acquired through their conquest. Unfortunately, they didn't take God's boundaries very seriously. They found loopholes in His instructions and through rebellion brought on themselves the fruit of their own disobedience. Because of their sin, they suffered a massive defeat in the next conquest campaign at Ai. Joshua cried out to God, "Why?!" God's answer says it all.

What happens when God gives you boundaries and you overstep them?

"Israel has sinned, and they have also transgressed [literally: overstepped] My covenant which I commanded them. For they have even taken some of the accursed things, and have both stolen and deceived; and they have also put it among their own stuff." (Joshua 7:11)

Sometimes after a major victory in our lives, we head into the next similar situation with great confidence. But we have to remember that our victory lies squarely in our obedience to God and His Word. It's not because we're so great that we find ourselves overcoming sin. Israel's problem in this passage was that they held onto some things from their enemy that God clearly told them to completely stay away from. They didn't fully obey. They were half-hearted in their response to God's boundaries, revealing their own pride and independence from God's instructions. Much like the thoughts that came to Eve in the garden, "God said this, but if I just do this one thing, it's okay." Because of Israel's disobedience and pride, they walked into the next battle with unrepented sin in their hearts, and they suffered a massive defeat.

Is there anything in your life that God has said was off-limits, and you have reasoned yourself out of obedience to that boundary? If there are things you have welcomed into your life that God has clearly told you to abstain from, watch out. There could be massive defeat ahead. And like Israel, you could find yourself surprised by that, crying out, "Why God?"

proper alignment

God loves boundaries. He's often really specific with them, as we can see throughout the Bible. One kind of boundary He makes available to us is that of an accountability relationship. Christians often talk about the importance of accountability, but many of us don't walk in it as fully as we should. An accountability relationship is a very intimate and special relationship that should not be entered into haphazardly. By giving someone permission to keep you accountable, you are making yourself vulnerable. You are giving another the right to speak into your life, which means that you want to make sure your accountability partners are living at a level where they hear from the Lord and can speak His truth to your situation.

I remember in college I heard a lot about friends of mine who had "accountability partners." I had never heard that term before. I thought that was a neat concept, but I didn't really understand how crucial it was at the time. In fact, I'd even venture to say that most of my college friends who were in such relationships didn't even really use them appropriately. It's all well and good to have peers keeping you accountable, but peers do

By giving someone permission to keep you accountable, you are making yourself vulnerable.

146

not complete God's picture of accountability. If you don't have anyone with spiritual authority over you keeping you accountable, you'll be missing an essential element in your development. Our pastor summed it up in the phrase "proper alignment." There are three elements of proper alignment. You have:

1. **People over you** with spiritual authority and wisdom to speak into your life (your parents, your pastor, and your church leaders are examples).

2. **People alongside you** to build the Kingdom with (this would be peers) who are present in your everyday life, and who can sharpen you with the way they live as well as with strong encouragement and truth.

3. **People below you** who you're pouring into (younger siblings, younger Christians, or those who God has drawn to seek your counsel). These people are not actually "below" you in God's order of importance. "Below" means they are seeking spiritual covering under the wisdom and authority God has given you thus far in life.

So you see, peer relationships are essential, but they are not the only element in keeping your life accountable and properly aligned spiritually. They are only one part of the picture.

During the critical years of maturity from teenage adolescence to young adulthood, you will be up against many situations that you have not encountered before. It's a season of new experiences and challenges, and you'll need mature accountability more than ever before. For one thing, those who are more mature and developed spiritually will have the courage to speak the truth even when it hurts. If you're struggling with a certain habitual sin, and your peer accountability partner does too, you may not find the same level of gut-wrenching honesty in her approach, but instead an abundance of mercy since she can relate to what you've

147

done. Not that your peers can't help bring conviction to your life, but often peers will be afraid to appear hypocritical, so they may not challenge you as strongly to repent because they feel guilty of the same sin.

With the young women I mentor, they know that I expect and give complete honesty in our relationship. Anything less than that is an insult to the trust they have placed in me. If I find that a woman I am mentoring is purposely leaving information out or trying to hide things from me, then our mentoring relationship is in jeopardy of continuing. I will call that woman on her deceit, and I will give her the opportunity to get right with the Lord and with me. If she doesn't want to do that, or if she says all the right things but doesn't have a heart of repentance, then she's really not ready for the level of relationship I am offering. Oh, how I have agonized over situations like these! But in the end I must accept the fact that I can't take her anywhere she refuses to go.

attitude is everything

Having the practical boundaries of rules and accountability in your life will help protect you from your own poor decisions. But they cannot prevent you from them entirely, because in every situation sin is your choice—yours and yours alone. Even a life hemmed in by boundaries can become eaten up with a rebellious heart. Maybe you come from a home where your parents were extremely strict and you had rules up the wazoo. I've seen both good and bad fruit come from strict homes, and the deciding factor is usually a young person's attitude, *not* the parents (aren't you surprised?).

One girl I know has two of the strictest parents I've ever met, but I have never heard her bad mouth her parents or complain. In fact, when

Rules, boundaries, and accountability that hurts at times...these things are not always fun.

she was given the choice to move into the dorms of the college a few blocks from her house, she chose to continue living at home to save money. Most people would have been out the door in a heartbeat, but this young lady had kept her heart right toward her parents. In fact, I will not be surprised in the least to watch her go on to be a huge success in her life because she has honored her parents as her spiritual authority, even when their rules may have seemed overwhelming to her at the time. "Honor your father and mother... that it may be well with you." (Ephesians 6:2-3)

Rules, boundaries, and accountability that hurts at times... these things are not always fun. Allowing yourself to be subject to the wisdom and authority of others may not always be an easy experience. If you don't guard your heart against rebellion, it won't matter what rules you do or don't keep. Your own rebellion will lead you down a path of stupidity before you know it.

For example, a young lady came to me once and asked me to keep her accountable in a certain area. I observed her life and met with her weekly. I saw several issues in her daily decisions that created very convenient loopholes to disobey the guidelines we had come up with to help her walk free. Being my blunt self, I confronted her on these loopholes and strongly encouraged her to cut off the behavior that I knew would only prolong her struggle. She sweetly said she'd consider what I said and thanked me for my "advice."

Every week it was the same, and her stories only got worse and worse about how she had fallen in sin. She was in bondage to that sin for nearly a decade, and it greatly derailed and delayed her destiny in the Lord. She had a rebellious heart, disguised in a sweet demeanor. She thought she had everyone convinced that her intentions were honorable (even herself). However, I didn't see her choosing obedience so she could find freedom. Her problem was not an issue of self-control, it was an issue of pride. Deep down, she thought she could figure it out herself.

This is important to understand. Submitting to another person's authority isn't simply asking them what they *think* about your actions or decisions. *Submitting* is actually being willing to walk in obedience to the biblical truth that a leader has challenged you with, even if it's the opposite of what your flesh wants. It's putting your trust in their wisdom concerning Biblical living, and giving weight to what they hear from the Holy Spirit concerning your situation. It's being mature enough to realize that this person may see things from a more clear and mature perspective than you do (especially if sin has deceived you). Going through the motions of "seeking counsel" is not going to help you one bit. Only if you *receive* the counsel with a humble heart and walk in scriptural obedience can you actually benefit from it.

Submitting to another person's authority isn't simply asking them what they think about your actions or decisions.

honor vs. dishonor

A beloved spiritual father said it to me this way, "If the decisions you make in your life take your leaders by surprise, you've dishonored that leadership." When a woman who I am mentoring and holding accountable in the area of relationships announces to the Internet world that she is in a relationship, one which I know nothing about, I immediately feel dishonored. I have set aside my time to help her, pray for her, and disciple her, so I should not be among the last to know of a major decision she has made (especially one that goes against the boundaries we have been talking about). That kind of behavior reveals that this young woman has not been honest with me and truly does not want to be held accountable. She may like the notion of accountability, but she's not willing to pay the price and make the sacrifices necessary for that accountability to bear fruit in her life.

I remember an old episode of "The Cosby Show" (ever heard of that? Bill Cosby?) where the second oldest daughter comes home from a trip to Africa, and while introducing the handsome man at her side to her parents, she announces that they eloped while she was gone. Her parents were shocked and mad. Cliff Huxtible, the father, explains it to his new son-in-law something like this: "It's like you just presented me with a steak dinner, but instead of it being on a plate, it's on a trash can lid." As a father, he was hurt by not being able to celebrate this major event in his daughter's life, or even weigh in on whether or not this man seemed worthy of marrying her in the first place.

When you are faced with decisions, especially ones that have life-changing consequences, the people you are close to should be the first to know about them (*before* you make them). When we were praying about our cross-country move, we talked with our closest friends and mentors first. We got their input, asked them to help us see past our own emotional influences one way or another, and spent time in prayer with them. We didn't just announce to them, "Well guys, we're moving." We needed their insight and prayer covering so we would make the choices that kept us in God's will. The perspective and prophetic insight from these people confirmed what God was showing us in our own hearts and gave us the confidence and courage to step out in faith to obey God.

That's why Proverbs 11:14 says, "In the multitude of counsel there is safety." God wants to keep you safe from making really bad choices. And if you are in a place spiritually where you lack clarity, He can help you by placing people in your life who can pray with you and call you back to the truth of Scripture.

A young woman announced to me her plans to go "clubbing" with some of her other Christian friends. I told her truthfully that I thought it was a horrible idea, and that she had nothing to gain from such an escapade. I also challenged her to find one leader in her life who would feel differently. A smart girl easily realizes an overwhelmingly unanimous response would mean that she wasn't looking at it accurately. I wish I could tell you she listened to the people in her life who wanted to love and protect her, but she didn't. Unfortunately, her "innocent" runs to the club with her "Christian" friends began a slow fade on her convictions and eventually led her out of God's will for a painfully long season.

God's ultimate authority

Submitting your life to the covering of spiritual authority does not mean you follow someone's counsel without consulting the Lord, or that you go against the Holy Spirit's leading in order to "obey" your leaders. Ultimately, God and His Word should be the final authority in your life.

For example, a young woman confessed a certain habitual sin to her pastor's wife, hoping that bringing it into the light would help her find freedom and a path toward healing. Unfortunately, the pastor's wife told the young lady that her sin wasn't so bad, and that she shouldn't feel like she needed to confess it every time she was struggling. Bad advice plunged that young woman into years of confusion as she battled what became a stronghold and an addiction. Thankfully, she sought the Lord about what the right thing was to do, and God led her out of that congregation into a very healthy church family where she could find healing. Later on, she learned that her previous pastor's wife had been struggling with the same sin, so of course she was of little help in finding freedom.

Not every person who has a designated place of "leadership" in your life will be able to lead you into spiritual health and growth. That's why it's critical that you know how to hear the voice of the Lord so you can discern who is leading a life worthy to lean into. Those people are out there. You may not see them in abundance where you are currently, but even if you just have one, God can use that one person tremendously to pour wisdom into you.

Leaders who are worth leaning into will have some distinguishing qualities about them. First, their life should consistently reflect biblical truth. If they advise you or anyone to do something that is not found in the Bible, that should be a red flag. Secondly, their life should have "fruit" that follows it. Scripture tells us that a good tree cannot bear bad fruit and vice versa (Matthew 7:17-18). You should be able to see a string of wisdom in that person's life that proves she is walking closely with the Lord. If you see ungodly attitudes, financial ruin, openly rebellious children, and jumping from job to job, that person is probably not suited to speak into your life at this time. Finally, good leaders are those who promote the welfare of others and who walk in humility. Beware of someone who is always trying to make her own name great.

put into action

It's important for you to identify the leaders in your life and to assess the covering that is available to you in them. There may be people who come to mind who you are not that close to, but who you sense are living a life of wisdom and would have a lot to pour into you. And there may be a person who you can identify as a leader in some capacity over you who is really not able to assist you in finding wisdom or in spiritual growth. Not every leader will have everything you need, but they should have something that contributes to your growth and brings health to your life in God.

List some of the leaders you can identify in your life right now. Think about what they contribute to your development, and list anything that comes to mind. (If "nothing" comes to mind, note that too).

1. _____

_____

2. _____

_____

3. _____

_____

Also, who can you call a partner—a peer who is not only in the same stage as you, but who is moving in the same direction—under the authority of God's truth? Beside each name, write how comfortable you are sharing areas of weakness with that person.

1. _____
   _____

2. _____
   _____

3. _____
   _____

When you get to the last chapter, you'll have an opportunity to learn more about how to pour into others as a leader and what that might look like.

"I would have lost heart, unless
I had believed that I would see
the goodness of the Lord
in the land of the living."

Psalm 27:13

chapter 9 smart girls never give up

perspective

Even if you were to do everything we've addressed in this book so far—if you know who you are in Christ, if you fear the Lord, if you guard your heart, if you cover yourself with amazing leaders—there is no guarantee that life will hand you roses. Sometimes life just stinks, and bad things happen, whether through the horrible choices of others or through unexplained sickness, tragedy, and the like. What then? What does wisdom look like when you are faced with something you never expected?

Most people are familiar with the story of Bethany Hamilton, a professional surfer who lost her arm in a shark attack when she was just 13 years old. Before the attack, it was clear to her family, friends, mentors, and surfing community that Bethany was on track to realizing her dream of turning pro. When she lost her arm, there was a collective sorrow that her promising future might not be realized. Although Bethany was a Christian and had a tenacious will to get back on the board, she naturally struggled with questions of "Why?" In the movie Soul Surfer, Bethany's character questions, "What happened to 'I can do all things'?" referencing the passage in Philippians 4:13, "I can do all things through Christ who strengthens me."

Dealing with the loss of a limb is challenging in all sorts of practical ways, but Bethany also faced tremendous emotional loss and fear about not doing what she loved because of it. One critical lesson came from her youth pastor who encouraged her to step back and get perspective. As a result, Bethany went on a life-changing trip to Thailand after the Tsunami in 2004. When she saw the ruin of an entire community, orphans, death and devastation, she had a very helpful perspective shift. And when she did return to surfing, her perseverance and faith in the face of a huge obstacle brought her international attention. She is no longer a young teenager with talent and a dream; she is a woman who understands that God has given her a message of hope and perseverance for the world. The way God has used Bethany's life to impact others is nothing short of amazing.[21]

Allow the Holy Spirit to give you perspective on what He can do in the midst of your suffering.

As you read this chapter, you may be facing difficult circumstances in your own life. I encourage you to allow the Holy Spirit to give you perspective on what He can do in the midst of your suffering.

gunned down

Anne Marie Hochhalter was a 17-year-old junior, who left English class on a typical high school day and settled outside for lunch with friends. Suddenly, sounds that mimicked popping balloons rang out, and Anne Marie felt a sharp pain in her back. She had been gunned down on a day that would live forever in the history books of school violence. Anne Marie almost became Columbine High School's fourteenth fatality on April 20, 1999 in Littleton, Colorado.[22]

The bullet that went into Anne Marie's back broke her vertebrae and caused her to be paralyzed from the waist down. She was also shot a second time that day, suffering punctures to her lung, liver, diaphragm, and a critical vein. She lay silently pretending to be dead, unaware that several of her classmates were being killed just one floor up in the library. Thankfully, paramedics arrived and rescued her amidst gunfire, rushing her to a nearby hospital.

Anne Marie's life was saved that day, but forever changed. The quiet clarinet player in marching band was forced to transform into a fighter, a survivor. There would be no more shrinking into the background. No more going unnoticed. The media frenzy about the Columbine shootings kept a careful distance during her four-month hospital recovery, but that would not last for long.

Anne Marie spent the entire summer in the hospital and was released right before school began—her senior year. The beginning of that year was filled with anxiety and loss as she transitioned from her hospital routine to everyday student life on the Columbine campus. Nothing was the same. She was in a wheelchair and unable to escape any amount of attention. As a paraplegic, she now needed help to do lots of things she could do before by herself. She had to learn to speak up and ask for people to notice and help her.

Then, before she even had a chance to catch her breath, Anne Marie was handed perhaps the most difficult situation a teenager could ever face. Just six months after she was shot, Anne Marie's mother committed suicide. Carla Hochhalter had already been struggling with depression and bipolar disorder before the Columbine shootings, and her condition worsened quickly in the aftermath. A few years later, Anne Marie told a reporter from *Rocky Mountain News*, "She was so sick. I can't hold it against her because mental illness is a terrible thing. In her mind, she thought it was the best thing she could have done."[23]

Anne Marie Hochhalter spent a few years reeling from the circumstances that had been handed to her. She did not bounce back one month, or even one year later. It took time. When Anne Marie was shot, she was a self-proclaimed atheist. But a few years later, as a young adult, she put her faith in Christ, and that was a profound shift in her progress. She cites a few things that I believe propelled her to a place of success and healing:

1. She found hope in the Lord.
2. She found a healing community of believers to support her emotional and spiritual growth.
3. She chose to forgive—the shooters and her mother.

490 times

Forgiveness is a biggie. There is no future hope for a woman who has been wronged unless she allows the Lord to do a deep work of forgiveness in her heart. It's not something that emerges out of emotional strength. It's a choice. It's a place to start from, and the Lord can do marvelous things in a life yielded to Him in forgiveness.

Your choice to forgive is one of the most powerful choices you have. With it you have the potential to completely destroy the enemy's plan for your life. He hates forgiveness. If you manage to survive the circumstances he's assaulted you with, he can still keep you bound to the pain as long as he can seize you with unforgiveness. But smart girls see that deception and refuse to take that bait. Forgiveness is the key to healing. The enemy knows that, and he wants to stop it! George Herbert, an Anglican priest from the 1600's said, "He who cannot forgive others destroys the bridge over which he himself must pass."

The first thing you must understand is that the miracle of forgiveness originates from God. He forgave you and me, and the entire world, of the sin that consumes our lives. He paid the ultimate price for that forgiveness by sending His only Son to the cross. If you are a Christian, that means you have repented of your sin and independence, and you have willingly received the forgiveness He extended to you. You won't be able to forgive others unless you understand that God forgives you *completely* (1 John 1:9).

Secondly, realize what forgiveness isn't. It's not forgetting the sin another has committed against you. Not remotely. Anne Marie is reminded every day as she maneuvers around her home in her wheelchair. There is no forgetting. She must live with the consequences of another person's sin every day. But only Anne Marie could choose to accept that, or else stay shackled to how unfair that reality is.

In forgiveness, there must be a resolve to remove yourself from the place of judgment. As long as you hold onto bitterness and anger toward someone who has sinned against you, you put yourself in the unrightful place of God, the only righteous judge. He has clearly told us in Scripture that vengeance belongs to Him and Him alone (Psalm 94:1). So often we punish people in our own minds, or trash them verbally to others because we don't like the fact that we aren't allowed to seek revenge. We would never openly *say* that, of course. But that's what it is. Forgiveness requires us to lay that attitude down. It means we cancel the debt that someone owes us. Not for their good, but for our good. I have learned first-hand... when I forgive someone, I am the person who is set free. Neil Anderson paints a memorable illustration in *Victory Over the Darkness*: "Take them off your hook and put them on God's hook."[24]

When I forgive someone, I am the person who is set free.

Lastly, understand that Jesus commands (not suggests) that we forgive (Matthew 6:14-15; Luke 6:37; Matthew 18:21-35; Mark 11:25,26). Therefore, unforgiveness in our lives is disobedience—sin. That may be hard for you to swallow, but it's true. You cannot get beyond the heartache unless you *deal with* unforgiveness as sin, repenting of it, and turning to a new way, the way of forgiveness.

Forgiveness is not easy. I know. I had to walk through an extremely painful season in my life where I was faced with the reality of needing to forgive someone whom I had loved, who had committed a horrible sin against my family. The consequences of the sin changed everything in my life. This person did not ask me for forgiveness or even acknowledge the consequences of the sin, which were quite public and downright humiliating to me. But God still required me to forgive. I had to choose whether or not I would walk into a hopeful future, or whether I would stay chained to the offense.

In studying Jesus' lesson on forgiveness in Matthew 18, we see a question about how many times we are to forgive another. Jesus' answer was seventy times seven. That's 490. That's a lot. Does that mean that we just sit back and let someone violate us that many times? Heck, no! Healthy boundaries are absolutely necessary to keep poisonous people from wounding you. Personally, I think it means you may need to choose forgiveness nearly 500 times, but it's still worth it. We are given a model prayer by Jesus in Luke 11, which includes taking time in prayer every day to forgive others. When you break it down numerically, an every-day-prayer for forgiveness for someone, 490 days in a row, equals roughly a year and four months. That's a good bit of time for God to heal your heart and shift your perspective. But it must start with a choice, one day at a time.

A woman of wisdom is most certainly a woman of forgiveness.

forgiving yourself

A new revelation came to me when I was 30 years old and completing the Freedom in Christ discipleship course. The final step of completion was praying through a series of strongholds to make sure you have closed the door to anything that would keep you from being all you are meant to be in Christ. When we got to the prayer section on forgiveness, we made a list of people we needed to forgive, and then we were encouraged to write "myself" at the bottom of the list.

Myself?

Sometimes you have no one to blame for the hellish place you find yourself in. Many women suffer and suffocate under the weight of the notion that they brought their pain on themselves. While that may be true to some degree, keep it in context of all you have learned in previous chapters about the nature of deception and temptation. Without a doubt, any woman's struggle with sin has an assignment from the enemy at its inception. Somewhere along the way she incurred damage from the consequences of the sin. And still in the midst of all the deception, she made choices that determined where it would end up. And no one is accountable for those choices except for her.

[handwritten margin note: Without a doubt, any woman's struggle with sin has an assignment from the enemy at its inception?]

I had never heard of forgiving myself. Could that have been the missing ingredient all those years when I was riddled in guilt over foolish things I had done? I never seemed to be able to move past the fact that I had brought so much pain on myself.

Think of forgiveness in terms of cancelling a debt, like Jesus taught in the passage we studied in the last section (Matthew 18). You may have screwed up royally, and there is nothing that you can do to even begin to put it right again. You may have completely derailed your life (thus far, it's never too late to get back on track), and you may feel like the debt owed is so insurmountable, that there is no sense in trying to fix it. In cases like these, many women throw in the towel and give in completely to the sin pattern, making it worse and worse.

Here's the thing with forgiveness toward anyone—you *can't* fix it. It's not yours to fix. Jesus took care of the debt on the cross. He cancelled your debt. No matter how much pain you have put yourself through by your own doing, He has already forgiven you. The key to accepting His forgiveness is repentance. "If we confess our sins, He is faithful and just to forgive us our sins and to cleanse us from all unrighteousness" (I John 1:9). If God, who is holy and perfect, can forgive you and cleanse you from *all* your sin, then surely you can forgive yourself for the things you've done. By the power of the Holy Spirit, you can be made new.

No matter how much pain you have put yourself through by your own doing, He has already forgiven you.

There is nothing you have done that God can't forgive and redeem... absolutely nothing.

out of the ashes

Forgiveness is your starting point. Understanding forgiveness in Christ for the things you've done and extending forgiveness to others, regardless of the pain, is where you begin. Wisdom must often emerge from the ashes of pain. Like springtime, wisdom can most assuredly penetrate the hardened soil of a passing winter. We are given no assurance as to the length of the winter, but we are promised that it is not forever. Weeping may endure for the night, but "joy comes in the morning" (Psalm 30:5). If you find yourself in that place of winter, know that the hope of springtime may be one step of obedience away. Proverbs 24:14 says, "Know also that wisdom is like honey for you: If you find it, there is a future hope for you, and your hope will not be cut off." (NIV)

For Nicole Braddock Bromley, her nine-year winter came to an abrupt end when she courageously shared a secret with her mother—her stepfather had been sexually abusing her repeatedly from age 5 to age 14. Nicole's mother believed her and reported it to the authorities, immediately taking her daughter into hiding. Seven days later, Nicole's stepfather committed suicide. Her winter had ended.

Out of the ashes of that horrific season, emerged a beautiful woman with a supreme mission to help other victims of sexual abuse. She could never have understood fully as a teenager the hope God was preserving for her. And she never would have made it into that future if she had not trusted Him for the strength to walk through each day. Although God did not fashion that horrible season of abuse in order to build Nicole's testimony, He most certainly used all of the pain she endured to build His Kingdom and destroy the works of the enemy. With great courage, Nicole wrote a book called, *Hush: Moving From Silence to Healing After Childhood Sexual Abuse*. This book beautifully illustrates the power of bringing secrets into the light.[25]

If the devil knew the redemptive impact Nicole's story would have, he would have never bothered her. Not only did his plan to ruin her life backfire, but her healing is multiplied as she helps countless others who are still living with the torment and shame of sexual abuse. Nicole is wreaking havoc on the kingdom of darkness as she helps people find freedom and hope by breaking their silence. Love it!

even when it's hard

Miriam was just 19-years-old when she attended a party with co-workers. She drank only a single glass of wine (legal in the country where she lived), yet she had no recollection of the rest of the night. Details from others helped her piece together events that led her to believe her drink had been spiked with a drug, and that she had been date raped by someone she knew. A few weeks later, she found out she was pregnant.

Although she was a born-again Christian and raised in a Christian family with strong values and beliefs, Miriam, in her despair, considered abortion. She said she was afraid her child would look like her rapist. She had made her mind up that abortion was the most compassionate choice, but then, with a hospital gown already on, God intervened. Miriam had a moment of clarity where she felt a sudden rush of God's love for her child, and she couldn't go through with it.

Carrying her baby full-term meant another hard choice: parenting or adoption. Miriam sensed that God wanted her to parent her child, despite the lifetime of sacrifice that would bring. She became a single parent at the age of 19. She chose to walk in obedience to the Lord's calling, even though it would be difficult.

Now she is in her late twenties and has a daughter who is eight years old and does indeed look like the man who raped Miriam. She says the love she feels for her child now far supersedes the love she felt for her the day she chose to keep her. Today, Miriam is a member of the British police force and is making a difference in her community and in the life of a precious little girl.[26]

Miriam gave God the opportunity to grow her through an unexpected and undeserved circumstance. Did God cause her to be raped so He could grow her? Certainly not! I'm sure He shared the tears she cried as she realized what had happened to her. But He did most certainly rescue her from a lifetime of regret and emotional trauma over an abortion.

My pastor has used this phrase many times, and it has changed my life: God is not committed to our comfort; He is committed to our growth. Countless times in Scripture we see those who are obedient to him suffer devastating circumstances. But we also see them being promoted, preserved, and rescued when they respond to the devastation appropriately. I think of Joseph in the Bible who was abandoned and sold into slavery by his brothers and spent years in prison for no good reason. Yet God had a plan of redemption, and He raised Joseph to a place of great influence (see Genesis 37–46). When we remain obedient to Him in the midst of the pain, He can and will turn the most difficult circumstances into pathways that lead to growth and triumph.

God is not committed to our comfort; He is committed to our growth.

keys to restoration

You, no doubt, have endured painful circumstances you had no control over. And you've probably created some of your own pain with different choices as well. Do you believe that God can redeem you and heal you no matter what has happened?

In the book of Joel, God sent judgment on the people of Israel for their own disobedience. His judgment was seen in swarms of locusts that consumed the land and the harvest. Yet, after the destruction, God gave them a promise—that He would restore the years the locusts had eaten. Your life could be in the midst of devastation this very moment. But there is nothing God can't restore. He is your hope, and His miracle-working power is available to you just like it is to all of the girls mentioned in this book so far. He doesn't love you any less, and you are not worth any less than they are.

There are some keys to restoration that are important to understand as you move forward. Look at Galatians 6:1: "Brethren, if a man is overtaken in any trespass, you who are spiritual *restore* such a one in a spirit of gentleness, considering yourself lest you also be tempted." The word restore in this passage is the Greek word "katartizo," which means to arrange, set in order, equip, adjust, complete what is lacking, make fully ready, repair, prepare. Notice the passage is directed to us as Christians in how we are to help others get back on track.

Key #1: You can't be restored in isolation; you need community.

Anne Marie Hochhalter found new momentum in her restoration process once she became part of a church community. Some may attend church and think it's the same thing, but it's not. You can't be equipped and made fully ready by people who don't know your wounds. The accountability we walked through in Chapter Three is a huge part of the restoration process, as well as the covering discussed in Chapter Eight.

I've been part of what I would call a "restoration team" a few times in my life, twice as a sister in the Lord to another woman who was in crisis and needing restoration, and once as that woman who was in crisis myself. I can't think of anything more powerful that a church can offer. A few women who are further along in their spiritual journey, or who have survived similar crises, led by a pastoral team member who can oversee the hurting person's spiritual development and prophetically speak into the situation. This is a safe place where wounds can be exposed and dealt with. It's not a griping session. It has the potential, if carefully put to the model of Scripture, to be exactly what Galatians 6 talks about as restoration. It is life-changing. You may not be able to conceptualize this kind of process at the church you're at. Ask God to lead you to know who the people might be who could walk you through such a process.

Key #2: You can't be restored unless you repent. If you are in a mess you created, restoration begins with repenting for disobedience to God's Word and will. Repentance is not just saying, "oops!" or "I'm sorry, God." It means actually *turning* from your sin. In Matthew 3:2, John the Baptist tells people "Repent!" A note in my Spirit-Filled Life Bible says, "Repentance is a decision that results in a change of mind, which in turn leads to a change of *purpose* and *action*."

God's goodness leads us to repentance (Romans 2:4), but godly *sorrow* is what actually produces repentance. If the weight of your sin and what it has done to separate you from God doesn't move you on some kind of emotional level, I question whether it's authentic (and by the way, so will others).

If you are in a mess someone else created, repentance may still be needed if you have committed the sin of trying to live independently of God or the sin of unforgiveness toward the other person. Ask the Holy Spirit to reveal to you if there is anything you need to repent of, and be prompt in speaking the words of repentance, asking God for His forgiveness to cleanse you from your sin. When you are clean before Him, you are poising yourself for an extreme outpouring of His favor and mercy on your situation. As much as it depends upon you, walk clean.

Key #3: There is no half-way in restoration. Ask anyone who is in the business of home restoration, it is a difficult, lengthy, and often painful process. There is no four-step fix-it-yourself "IKEA®" solution in home restoration. Great attention is given to the details. Materials are chosen to most closely replicate the original materials used. When a home is fully restored, it looks like it has been completely rebuilt, only with the original character and structure in place. It is strong and ready to last.

Restoration doesn't mean changing who you are. It means your unique God-designed features are now strengthened and able to withstand the harsh elements you will encounter in life. During my restoration, I had people looking into my life saying, "This attitude has to go," or "This is an area of disobedience." I had to be willing to gut those things out of my life and allow them to be replaced by God's true character. It was not easy! It's almost as if I had a staircase railing that I loved in my house, but it was rotting from the inside out. What if I had been unwilling to part with it because I was so used to it and couldn't imagine anything else in its place? It would have been dangerous to keep a railing that could fail me one day, causing me to stumble down the flight of stairs and injure myself or others. I would need to be willing to let it go. In the same way, I had to see the renovation process of my heart through the eyes of the designer, the one who sees all the potential (God). I had to be willing to give up *anything* in order to have the structure of my heart become strong.

Restoration does not take a month. It often takes a year or more! And things could be really messy in the process. Stick with it. Don't take the scaffolding down outside because you just get too embarrassed with people knowing how much work there is to be done. Yield to the process; see it through to the end. There is a beautiful work of redemption on the other side, and it is worth any amount of humility and patience you can pay!

Smart girls never give up.

anything in order to have the structure of my heart become strong. I had to be willing to give up

170

put into action

Whether you find yourself in the midst of difficult circumstances due to someone else's choices, or due to the poor choices you have made, there is a response to the pain that is full of wisdom. Forgiveness is your starting point. Ask the Lord who you need to forgive, and write those names down (in the space below, or on another sheet if you need more room). Don't forget about the need to forgive yourself as well.

""Does not wisdom cry out,
And understanding lift up her voice?
She takes her stand on the top of the
high hill, Beside the way, where the paths meet.
She cries out by the gates, at the entry
of the city, at the entrance of the doors..."
Proverbs 8:1-3

chapter 10
smarter, wiser

pursue wisdom

Well, young ladies, I cannot tell you how much I have loved pouring out my heart in the pages you have just read. I do not write these things to hear my own voice. I have written these things because of the intense love and burden I have for your generation. God has commanded me to be part of your journey, anyone who will listen. I truly feel called by God to come alongside you and help lead you into womanhood with wisdom and truth. I hope this book has challenged you to see the importance of wisdom and the power of the choices you make every day.

As we bring our journey together to a close, let me encourage you on a few final things. *Pursue* wisdom; go after it; run your heart out to gain it. You have no excuse to be stupid after reading this book. No matter what you may think of my observations and instruction, you can't ignore the truth of God's Word that has been laid out before you. (Well, you totally could, actually, but that would not be so smart now would it?)

Proverbs says wisdom cries out loudly to us. Wisdom is like a loud woman in the middle of the street—you can't ignore her! She wants to be noticed. She will do anything to get your attention. Aren't you glad that when God told you to get wisdom, He wasn't talking about some hide-and-seek game where you might find her or you might not? He made wisdom loud, conspicuous, and easy to locate. Wisdom has cried out to you in the pages of this book and in the pages of your Bible. Can you hear her?

change is a-comin'

If you find yourself challenged by the lessons you've learned in this material so far, then you better prepare yourself to welcome change into your life. Once you know what it is you need, God will hold you accountable to act on the knowledge you've gained. Wisdom is the application of knowledge. It means nothing to just "know" things unless you use that information to improve your life and the lives of others around you.

I dare you to pray about what changes you need to make in your life in order to move to a greater place of wisdom. Think about what you've learned in each chapter.

- Chapter One: Live on purpose instead of living randomly.
- Chapter Two: Get honest about your spiritual gaps.
- Chapter Three: Realize stupidity has a high price.
- Chapter Four: Walk in the fear of the Lord, understanding temptation and deception.
- Chapter Five: Know who you are in Christ, and find your significance only in Him.
- Chapter Six: Take the long view of life, and handle small choices well.
- Chapter Seven: Guard your heart concerning boys and romance.
- Chapter Eight: Lean into leaders and live in the blessing and protection of spiritual covering.
- Chapter Nine: Never give up, even in the midst of trials.

Change is not always easy. Sometimes change needs to be radical in order to be free from the lure of temptation. The Bible says to *flee* youthful lusts (2 Timothy 2:22). Remember Dr. Wanda Turner, the woman I wrote about who referred to you as a diamond? She would say, "In other words, run baby, run! Change your phone number, move away and leave no forwarding address!" There is no point in entertaining things in your life that lead you into the pit of stupidity. If the friends you have entice you to do things you know are wrong, then they aren't really friends. Do you think God is big enough to bring you new friends who would support the changes you're making to pursue wisdom? You bet! He already knows what you need, and He is well able to provide the answer. But you'll have to step out in faith and show that you are serious about getting smart.

[handwritten margin note: There is no point in entertaining things in your life that lead you into the pit of stupidity]

Take a few minutes and ask the Lord which things in your life need to change in order for you to walk smarter and wiser. It could include things like relationships you need to sever or a renewed commitment to walk in humility toward your parents as your spiritual covering. You might want to ask a trusted leader to join you in prayer as you consider these things. Write down the changes God reveals to you here.

1. _____

2. _____

3. _____

Now, think about who you can talk to about these changes. Who will help keep you accountable in the new direction God wants

SMART GIRL, stupid world

you to head? You can't get there on your own. You need help from your leaders and your covenant comrades. List three people in your life who can keep your feet walking the road of wisdom as you make positive changes in your journey.

1. _____

2. _____

3. _____

fear of man

As you move forward from this point, you will feel some support from other people, and probably some opposition too. You might find yourself tempted to shrink back when faced with the opinions of others. The Bible calls this the "fear of man." Listen to the warning in Proverbs 29:25. "The fear of man brings a snare, but whoever trusts in the Lord shall be safe."

Saundra, my closest friend growing up, gave her life to the Lord at the age of 14, but her mom was not so crazy about the idea. In fact, Saundra often had to endure insults such as "goodie-two-shoes." That wasn't fun, believe me. But I watched my friend honor her mother despite the terrible attitude and rude comments that came over the years. She wasn't going to be swayed from the faith she had found. She wasn't afraid of her mother's comments, and she didn't give in to the bait they provided for anger. Saundra's mom took a long time to see things from the right perspective, but eventually, she gave up on trying

Proverbs 29:25 "The fear of man brings a snare..."

to talk her daughter out of being a Christian. And ultimately, just days before her death, Saundra's mom committed her own life to the Lord.

What if Saundra had cowered under her mom's disapproval? What if she had been afraid to stand up for the truth? Remember, the fear of man is a snare. It's a trap! If Saundra had abandoned her faith under the criticism of her mom, not only would she have been robbed of salvation, but her mother would have, too. Saundra stayed strong, and her decision to follow Christ is now propelling her own children into strong relationships with the Lord. Her story is a perfect example of how your choices can positively impact the generations to follow you.

Look at the changes you just listed in the previous section. If those things are really directed by the Lord, then you must obey Him. This is your first exercise in walking in the fear of the Lord. Do not fall into the fear-of-man trap, no matter what others may think of your new direction. Most likely, the people you find yourself around right now (other than your immediate family) may not be even remotely part of your life in five years. Don't abandon a glorious future for some momentary criticism from those who are not part of your journey.

Is there anyone in your life whose opinion of you and your choices could weaken your resolve for change? List anyone who comes to mind, and commit to pray about your relationship with that person, asking God to help you overcome your fear.

1. _____

2. _____

3. _____

finding the answer

You may be thinking that one day, when you're older, all this wisdom stuff will come naturally to you. Let me assure you by my observations that this is not the case. There are people way older than myself who certainly do not "get it." Wisdom is not something that grows naturally; you must obtain it.

I didn't write this book because I have all the answers and I plan to pass them down to you so you'll know what to do in every situation. I simply asked God to show me some of the main tools and truths that are available to *all* of us in Scripture so I can point them out to you and challenge you to use them in your journey toward wisdom.

Just as important as knowing the answer, is knowing how to *find* the answer. When I taught my son how to add and subtract, he approached it as a memorizing feat. He would get so upset when he couldn't remember the correct answer. I had to teach him *how* to find the answer if he couldn't remember it. It's the same way with God. He has given us lots of answers in the Bible, but there may be times when we aren't sure what the Bible says about something or where to even look for it. That's why we're given the tools to find God's answers! We have the Holy Spirit, who is called our helper; plus pastors, leaders, and Christian friends in our community who can point us to what the Word says and encourage us to follow the truth. We even have technology at our fingertips to search for just about any topic in the Bible. So when you're not sure what wisdom looks like in a certain situation, you can count on God to help you find the answer as long as you are asking Him for that help.

Wisdom is not something that grows naturally; you must obtain it.

pay it forward

Okay, this is the part where I get to talk about something that is seriously exciting. In the first chapter I talked about how God's plan for wisdom is that it be passed down from generation to generation, but that most people don't see that modeled for them. Here's where I get to challenge you to pay it forward.

Jesus commanded us to "make disciples" as some of His last words to us. If you become a parent, your primary disciples are your children. You will be responsible for their spiritual development and maturity. The only thing you are not responsible for is whether or not they will choose to follow Christ as Lord. That is their choice alone.

Yes, parenting is one of God's primary ways of paying wisdom forward to the next generation. But what about those who aren't parents? You may be a long way off from starting a family of your own. Do you wonder how to pay it forward in the season you're in right now? I know some amazingly wise women in their 40's and 50's who are either unmarried or without children of their own. What about them; how do they pay it forward?

Besides our own biological and adopted children, God brings us spiritual children as well. As you mature into your adult years, my prayer is that you would be inspired to be a spiritual mother of sorts to other young ladies who will need the wisdom of the lessons you have learned up to that point. The women I mentioned above who are without natural children all have rich and enduring legacies with spiritual children. They are constantly pouring their lives out to benefit younger generations or new believers. They are living the heart of God's plan for wisdom—passing it on.

No matter what age or stage you are in right now, God is preparing you to disciple others. No Christian is exempt from this mandate Jesus gave us. He didn't say, "Hey, all of you guys who become pastors or teachers, make disciples." His call to discipleship is for all of us. His perfect plan is for each of us to take our place in the discipleship matrix, to strengthen other less-mature believers.

You may not feel ready to mentor or disciple another girl. You may be just walking out of a season of stupidity where your choices brought a lot of heartache. It's okay; don't feel the pressure to immediately pour into others until you are at a place of stability. The Bible says those who teach shouldn't be novices (1 Timothy 3:6), so you may need some time to mature. But be thinking and praying about what it will look like when you do get to a place of stability, where your life is bearing the fruit of wisdom.

I watched one young lady who I mentored get a clear picture from the Lord about how she was to help disciple her younger sisters who were struggling. With five years difference in their age, it was the perfect fit for her to pass on the things she had learned the hard way during her early twenties.

If you are a senior in high school, you might ask God to show you a 7th or 8th grader who needs your support, encouragement, and wisdom. If you are in college, perhaps opportunities await you to be part of high school campus ministry where you can mentor younger women. You don't have to have everything they need, it wouldn't be God's design for that to happen anyway. But you have *something* they need. You remember what it was like to walk in their shoes, and you have a sense of the mountains they will face as they approach the next stage of life. You've digested a lot of truth in the pages of this book, and you've been pointed to a lot of Scripture. My hope is that these things would be weapons on your tongue, ever ready to help a younger friend stay away from the world's stupidity.

staying humble

The more you learn about God's ways of wisdom, the more momentum your life will gain. You will find relationships are more fruitful, and you will experience the blessing of promotion and success as your "smart girl" skills develop.

Let me give you one word of caution. Stay humble. Recognize that God is the source of whatever measure of wisdom you may walk in. You might see others making mistakes, and you will be tempted to view them through the eyes of judgment, as if you are superior to them for not making those same poor choices. Remember, pride always leads to your destruction (Proverbs 18:12). As much as I hope you make great choices and follow God's truth to build a life of wisdom, I also hope you will see struggling women around you with the compassion of Christ. They may not know the hope of the gospel—share it with them. They may not see themselves as valuable, making them unable to recognize their unhealthy habits in reaching for significance. Speak value to those women. Ask God to help you see and love others the way He sees and loves them.

You don't have to have everything they need, it wouldn't be God's design for that to happen anyway. But you have something they need.

When I was a teenager, I had so much pride in my own virginity that I couldn't see people accurately who had already had sex. I didn't see the hurts they carried from the failed attempts to feel loved or satisfy their desires. I had so much pride, I wasn't vigilant enough in guarding my own heart and mind from temptation when the time came. I thought I was indestructible. My own virgin pride caused me to be blind to the reality that

I was just as vulnerable to sin as other people, and I could be easily swayed when I allowed myself to get too emotionally attached in relationships. Eventually, my vulnerability took center stage, and I became shocked at my own lustful desires!

When I mentor young ladies, there are often lots of skeletons that need to come out of the closet right up front. The mistakes of their pasts are met with the utmost grace and mercy as we begin our relationship. And as they are finding their way to a new place of spiritual growth, there are always pitfalls and setbacks that need to be talked through and processed. Again, there is much grace. This young woman is still learning how to walk the narrow road.

This might be a gross analogy to you, but it's kind of like potty training children (stay with me, now). At first, you are giving lots of instruction and encouragement; you are happy just to have them realize they just pooped in their pants. The next phase is helping them realize how nice it is to have dry, clean underwear. They're rewarded for staying dry. And finally, the rewards from Mommy go away as they learn to take care of their own bodily functions. The reward now is just being a member of the big-girl-club and being able to listen to their own bodies. But what do you do when your child refuses to poop on the potty and says things like "You can't make me!" The attitude has to be disciplined. If they refuse to learn how to poop on the potty and they turn four, then five, then six... well, that's just wrong. The grace you gave them at the beginning when they were learning the ropes is gone. Now, they are dealing with your very tough love to teach them the right thing, and trust me, after six years of diapers you would be one desperate woman to get them to learn that lesson!

When you are walking life out with others, you may see them make mistakes that frustrate you. At first, you are called to gently help them learn and grow to the next phase of their development. If they continue to flounder, your approach may need to grow more direct. If after a prolonged season someone you know refuses to grow or receive truth, you need to pray about whether your relationship with them is fruitful. I'm not saying you automatically cut them off, but you need to know what God thinks about it, and seek counsel from others who can help you see His perspective objectively. It's possible you don't have a place to speak into their life anymore, and you may need to pull back and just pray. That's exercising humility.

When you walk in humility toward others, you will understand the reality that you are just as vulnerable to sin as they are.

When you walk in humility toward others, you will understand the reality that you are just as vulnerable to sin as they are. It doesn't mean you can't still take a stand against sin. There are friendships in my life that are now at a distance because clearly that person does not want to live their life God's way, and they aren't interested in whatever encouragement I may have to offer otherwise. I'm not going to chase them down with the truth, but I'm not going to look down on them either. My responsibility before the Lord is to pray for them and to have healthy boundaries in place to keep my family and myself from being negatively affected by their sinful choices. And I remind myself that if it weren't for the grace of God, I would probably be in their same shoes and much worse. It helps me to see them accurately, and it motivates me to pray for them. One of the greatest joys I have ever experienced was seeing someone who I thought was long gone yield herself fully to Christ and find forgiveness and healing for the things she had done. *Lord, help me to be patient with others as they grow, just like you are patient with me.*

put into action

You may have been handed some deficits; you may have endured some painful consequences, but you can grow in wisdom from any starting place. Any amount of wisdom you gain will mean nothing unless you have yielded your life to Christ, repented from your sin and independence, and declared your dependence on Him. Without Christ, there is not one thing you could do that will matter eternally. With Christ, there is forgiveness of sin to any length, and even the smallest steps of obedience bring Him honor and glory throughout generations.

If you haven't dedicated your life to Christ, if you haven't been saved from your sin, you have that chance now. If you think you might be saved, but you're not sure, why not settle it once and for all?

Below are some Scriptures and a model prayer you can pray all by yourself, but I highly encourage you to find a Christian friend or leader to be with you when you do. There is something supernatural that happens when we agree with each other in prayer. Praying a prayer of salvation is a life-changing moment, and inviting someone to be part of that moment is one of the greatest blessings you could give them. It will also help build accountability into your new born-again life from its first breath. I can't think of a better way to start fresh.

Scriptures to read: (Don't be lazy now, this is your eternal life we're talking about! Go ahead and look them up.)

- John 3:16
- Romans 3:23
- 1 John 2:2
- Romans 6:23
- Romans 10:9-10

prayer of salvation

Dear God, thank you for loving me enough to send your only Son, Jesus, to bring me eternal life. I realize that my sin and trying to do things my own way have separated me from your love and caused my life great pain. I am making a conscious decision to turn from my sinful ways, and I want to thank you for paying the debt of my sin through Jesus so I could find forgiveness and be reconciled back to you. I believe Jesus died on the cross and triumphed over death through resurrection; and I believe He did it for me. I want a new start on life; I want to be born-again and live for you, God. I invite your Holy Spirit to live in my heart, helping me obey you and grow in my understanding of you. I declare this day that I will live for you and follow your plan for my life, with your help and leading. In Jesus Name, Amen.

Young lady, if you prayed that prayer, you are now on a road that leads to real fulfillment. God's abundant life can now knock your socks off as you serve and grow in Him. What a beautiful thing!

Your next steps are learning to grow in your daily devotion to God through attending a healthy church, reading the Bible, prayer (just talking to Him and listening, nothing fancy or religious), worship (expressing devotion to Him), and fellowship (building relationships with other Christians – you need them!). I also encourage you to learn some of the basics of what life in God is about through resources such as:

- *So You're Born Again...Now What?: A New Believer's Guide To Kingdom Living*; Written By: Karen Wilson Vatel

- *Start (NKJV): The Bible for New Believers*, New Testament Edition; Edited By: Greg Laurie

good-bye

I am almost in tears as I write these final sentences. Obeying God to write these words to you has been one of the greatest journeys of my life. I pray your life will be full of wisdom and purposeful living. I pray you will overcome the stupid lies of the world and the devil, and that you will help others to do the same. I pray you will walk as the smart girl God created you to be.

"Therefore I also, after I heard of your faith in the Lord Jesus and your love for all the saints, do not cease to give thanks for you, making mention of you in my prayers: that the God of our Lord Jesus Christ, the Father of glory, may give to you the spirit of wisdom and revelation in the knowledge of Him, the eyes of your understanding being enlightened; that you may know what is the hope of His calling, what are the riches of the glory of His inheritance in the saints, and what is the exceeding greatness of His power toward us who believe, according to the working of His mighty power..." (Ephesians 1:15-19)

endnotes

chapter 1

1. Barna, George. *Transforming Children Into Spiritual Champions*. Ventura: Gospel Light, 2003.

2. Anderson, Neil. *Victory Over The Darkness*. Ventura: Regal Books, a division of Gospel Light, 2000.

chapter 2

3. www.shellylubben.com

chapter 3

4. Morrison, Keith. "A Fugitive Turns Herself in After 12 Years." *Dateline NBC*, February, 2006. (http://www.msnbc.msn.com/id/9766179/ns/dateline_nbc/t/fugitive-turns-herself-after-years/#.T9UijxzSRWA)

5. St. George, Donna and Stein, Rob. "Number of Unwed Mothers has Risen Sharply in U.S." *Washington Post*, May 14, 2009.

6. www.naccrra.org; National Association of Child Care Resource & Referral Agencies (NACCRRA)

7. Doherty, Shawn. "Rates of STDs Among Teens Reach Epidemic Levels." *The Capitol Times*, January 6, 2010.

8. Howard, Kate. "Cops Say Unraveling Life Led Kazemi to Kill McNair, Self." *The Tennessean*, July 9, 2009.

chapter 4

9. *Spirit Filled Life Bible: New King James Version*. Nashville: Thomas Nelson, 1991.

10. Groeschel, Craig. *The Christian Atheist: Believing in God but Living as If He Doesn't Exist*. Grand Rapids: Zondervan, 2010.

chapter 5

11. Anderson, Neil. *Victory Over The Darkness*. Ventura: Regal Books, a division of Gospel Light, 2000.

12. Palagyi, Zsa Zsa. "Kristen Anderson: Suicide Interrupted." The 700 Club. (http://www.cbn.com/700club/features/amazing/Kristen_Anderson_120407.aspx)

13. Anderson, Neil. *Victory Over The Darkness*. Ventura: Regal Books, a division of Gospel Light, 2000.

chapter 6

14. Foxnews.com. "Disgraced Miss Nevada USA Katie Rees Asks for a Second Chance After Being Stripped of Her Crown." December 25, 2006. (http://www.foxnews.com/story/0,2933,238513,00.html)

15. Starr, Colleen. "Former Miss Nevada Katie Rees Vs. Miss California Carrie Prejean." *Examiner.com*, May 13, 2009. (http://www.examiner.com/article/former-miss-nevada-katie-rees-vs-miss-california-carrie-prejean)

16. Stenzel, Pam. "Sex Has A Price Tag" *(DVD)*. Straight Talk; www..pamstenzel.com.

chapter 7

17. Moore, Farrar. *From Hurt to Hope*. Nashville: Caring Resources, 2007,

18. Anderson, Neil. *Victory Over The Darkness*. Ventura: Regal Books, a division of Gospel Light, 2000.

19. www.cdc.gov

chapter 9

20. Hamilton, Bethany, Bundschuh, Rick and Berk, Sheryl (Contributor). *Soul Surfer: A True Story of Faith, Family, and Fighting to Get Back on the Board*. New York: Pocket Books, a division of Simon & Schuster, 2004.

21. Weeks, Linton. "Moving On After Columbine: Thoughts Of A Survivor." *www.npr.org*; April 20, 2009. (http://www.npr.org/templates/story/story.php?storyId=103287016)

22. Bartels, Lynn. "A Story of Healing and Hope." *Rocky Mountain News*, April 20, 2004.

23. Anderson, Neil. *Victory Over The Darkness*. Ventura: Regal Books, a division of Gospel Light, 2000.

24. Braddock Bromley, Nicole. *Hush: Moving from Silence to Healing after Childhood Sexual Abuse*. Chicago: Moody Publishers, 2007.

25. White, Hillary. "Rape Victim says God Granted a 'Rush of Love' for her Unborn Child Moments before Abortion." *Lifesitenews.com*, September 11, 2009.

Made in the USA
Charleston, SC
15 July 2013